Have  Your Way With Bureaucrats

Also by James Boren:
When in Doubt, Mumble

The
Layman's Guide
to
Pyramiding
Featherheads
and
Other
Strange
Birds

HAVE
YOUR WAY
WITH
BUREAUCRATS

James H. Boren

CHILTON BOOK COMPANY   Radnor
Pennsylvania

Copyright © 1975 by James H. Boren
First Edition   *All Rights Reserved*
Published in Radnor, Pa., by Chilton Book Company
and simultaneously in Ontario, Canada,
by Thomas Nelson & Sons, Ltd.
Designed by William E. Lickfield
Manufactured in the United States of America

Library of Congress Cataloging in Publication Data
Boren, James H.
   Have your way with bureaucrats.

   1.   Bureaucracy—Anecdotes, facetiae, satire, etc.
I.   Title.
JF1601.B66   1975   350'.001'0207   74-31053
ISBN   0-8019-5953-5

Foreword

This book does not deal with the concerted battle of a people against the massive bureaucratic movement, but it does nudge up to some of the small battles that an individual citizen may win. This book is a fun book. It was fun to write and fun to doodle. I hope it will bring some smiles—and perhaps a tear or two—to the faces of its readers who may even find a bit of haunting profundity behind the smiles.

The sketches in the book are the outgrowth of many years of academic, corporate, and governmental doodling. The use of my Latin American nickname, Vago de los Ríos, is the result of a familial compromise. My father, Dr. James B. Boren, a great man with a matching sense of humor, is a builder of colleges and universities and a great inspirer of men and women. I promised him that I would not use James Boren to identify the doodler of the birds, some of which may depict mutual friends. They would never admit to the behavioral patterns anyway.

My delightful, charming, and gracious mother, who has never seen some of the birds I have seen, was shocked when she saw me doodling the retiring nightingale. When she sees the moderated rendition of the streaking jaybird, she can hide behind the name of Vago de los Ríos.

A cousin, James E. Boren, and another cousin, Jodie Boren, are outstanding painters specializing in western art. We made an agreement by which I would not ruin their market and reputation by painting or sculpting under the name, Boren, and they would not take up professional mumbling. To my Aunt "Buttermilk Mae" (Mae Axton), who wrote "Heartbreak Hotel" and many other songs as well as a book, and to her son, my cousin, Hoyt Axton, who wrote "Joy to the World", "When the Morning Comes," and many other songs, I promised to demusicate my birds. The tunes the birds sing may be familiar to the readers, but they have not yet been put to music.

To Uncle Lyle who has long spoken of the genera of bureaucrats; to Uncle Woodrow who helped research *Mother Goose*, *Grimm's Fairy Tales*, and *Dick and Jane* for bureaucratic tendencies; to Cousin Susan who mumbled over the pages; to Cousin David whose oratory matches Demosthenes and whose ability will lead Oklahoma out of the bureaucratic wilderness; to my teacher-sons, Richard Vincent and James Stanley, who cautiously suggested a few birds; to Baby Sister Marilyn who has consistently spotted acabu birds at the drop of a memo; to Brother Gene who fights the good fight in a governmental agency that he prefers I not name; to Laurence and Irene Peter who analyzed the impotency of some of the incompetent birds; to Bob Culbertson who taught me how to analyze the residuals of State Department policies; to the orchestrators of the Leigh Bureau who have kept me mumbling on the lecture circuit; to Mike Hamilton who pursued me with paper in hand; to Benton Arnovitz of Chilton who patiently and questioningly guided my fanciful flights; to Geoffrey Dean, a delightful Canadian who knows how to market books; to the men of the Nixon White House who inspired me to mumble while in a state of shock; to Wade Fleetwood of Fleet's Inn, the Beachcomber, and some mumbling agency; to Harden and Weaver, marvelous marathon mumblers of Washington; to my partner in Mumbles Limited, Peter Gamble, noted network mumbler; to Jack King, the aviatory bureaucrat of Allegheny; to Corn, Padilla, Ritter, Nicholson, Johnston, Carpentier and Howard for inspiration; to the many other birds with whom I have roosted, hovered, and profundicated; and

Most of all, to my beautiful and lovely wife, Irene, who gave me encouragement when it was needed, and who cryingly smiled while I cluttered the nest with paper, ink, note-taking envelopes, and scraps of paper.

To all of them, and to my banker, Bill Sanford, a special thanks!

—Vago de los Ríos

Contents

Introduction

Taxes and death have long been recognized as two elements of life that have a sobering impact on the human spirit. Functioning before, during, and after the processes of taxes and death, however, is a third force that is increasingly impinging upon the daily lives of people from the Yukon to Tierra del Fuego and from Washington, Ottawa, and London, to Johannesburg, Brasilia, and Moscow. It is a force slowly growing and spreading intertwining tentacles that nutritionally embrace all of humanity with squiddistic tenderness. It is bureaucracy, the ultimate consumer.

Citizens may cry in anguish as they provide the nutritional fluids on which bureaucracy thrives, but the response to the cries and tears of citizens is limited to election-year oratory by those who provide, partake, and primly protest.

Are the anguished cries of citizens the only means of expressing concern that is open to them? Is there no great battle plan that can enable people to join together in a major effort to reverse the growth process of their bureaucratic institutions? Is there no action that an individual citizen can take to alter the growth of bureaucracy?

What an exciting possibility for a science fiction writer! But, alas! the story may be written some day, not in the pages of a science fiction book but in some historical journal.

Therefore, let us pack our treasured clichés in a light knapsack, and take an easy walk through the land of neuralgia, backaches, and pains.

Let us philosophize about bureaucracy and its shuffling artisans. Let us learn how to know a bureaucrat when we see one—as projected in the maximized minimality of linear relationships and as stereotypically conceptualized. Let us go forth in search of the fountains that bubble a happy juice—a juice that may not give eternal youth but one that can wash bitterness from our eyes and permit us to smile while we cry.

—James H. Boren

"There Is Something About A Bureaucracy"

There is something about a bureaucracy . . .
   The shuffling and twiddling sounds
That are blended in serious merriment
   With messages almost profound.
There are new regulations to amplify
   With fuzzified words and intent;
There are marginal thoughts to express with care,
   And rules by the millions to print.
There are memos to write and the drafts to clear,
   And papers all stacked in great piles;
There are coffee breaks, seminars, forms and phones,
   Procedures, committees, and files.
There are papers to shuffle and stamps to stamp;
   And doodles to doodle with skill.
There're initials to scrawl in a hurried style
   With circles that end in a frill.
Yes, there's something about a bureaucracy
   That orchestrates total delight,
But there's nothing to match the true bureaucrat
   Who mumbles by day and by night.

Part I

BUREAUCRACY AND THE BUREAUCRAT

Chapter 1

The Essence of Bureaucracy

In its early years of development, bureaucratic endeavors were conceived, born, and nurtured in much the same manner as they are today. Bureaucrats have always been pressed close to the public breast; they have been wrapped in the protective swaddling clothes of red tape; and they have prospered in the procedural abstractions and the torpid flow of paper that have confused nonbureaucrats through the ages.

The essences of bureaucracy can be sensed in many forms and through many techniques: creative non-responsiveness to the needs and interests of citizens; the avoidance of issues through the use of orbital dialogues; the postponement of decisions; the reliance on committees and clearances; the deft delegation of problems; the diffusion of responsibility; the proliferation of organizational entities and procedures; the production and shuffling of forms, memoranda, and reports; and mumblistic adherence to the creative status quo. All are essential elements of the dynamic inaction of bureaucracy.

Understanding the constituent elements of bureaucracy may give some insights into goals and processes, but the configuration is not complete until the student of bureaucracy can capture the inner spirit of the movement. The inner spirit of bureaucracy lies in the exciting interplay of nonideas and the effervescent sparkling of human personalities engaged in nondirective pursuits.

Bureaucracy is not the domain of any particular group or institution, neither is it simply a collection of techniques and procedures. BUREAUCRACY IS A WAY OF LIFE!

Bureaucrats express their professionalism and their life style in a variety of ways, but they do it with more resonance than logic and more artistry than art. As they become more competent bureaucrats through their interplay with citizens, they learn to paint and weave, dance and sing, thrum and mumble. They receive inspiration from each other as they move through time and tape to express the bureaucratic wisdom of the ages with memorable mumblings.

The paintings of Rembrandt, Renoir, and Picasso, for example, may appear as simple renditions when compared to the works of bureaucrats who can translate simple ideas into complex patterns, and small thoughts into big pictures. Few practitioners of the bureaucratic art can surpass a former President of the United States, who was a master in answering simple questions in press conferences with big-picture commentaries that were expressed through complex ministrokes. By putting questions in "proper perspective," bureaucrats can perimetize their pictures, sketch strawmanistic options, and paint candid generalities with star-spangled strokes.

Experienced bureaucratic artists are masters in swinging their brushes with forcefulness and style, and they can create images of optimal nothingness for puzzled citizens to behold. Though the pigments may be cocktailian and the olives may be twisted and dried, the oils of the oiled ones give permanency to the little messages of the big pictures.

4

The great tapestries of ancient temples and palaces are timid efforts when compared to the artistry of bureaucrats when they are inspired to serenely but lovingly weave red tape into the wrapping cloth of a society.

The outstanding prima donnas of bureaucracy move with nimble-footed grace from administration to administration with only an occasional nosistic glance at their public. Today, some vocalists still sing their watergatian arias with voices that reach the heights of ineffability or plumb the depths of nocturnal intonations.

As Rome was not built in a day, neither was the full range of artistic expression developed in a few years. It has taken centuries for bureaucrats to develop the art of doing nothing while appearing to be doing much. It is from this heritage that each new bureaucrat can draw inspiration until individual mastery can be accomplished.

Consider, for example, the spinning and whirling of a nonprofit organization whose chief claim to fame is its annual awards banquet. (Between the annual banquets, there are numerous reports and press releases that announce the only thing unveiled at the banquet.) The leadership of the organization includes some of the wealthiest businessmen of the nation and many of the best-known clergymen.

Large amounts of money are spent for surveys, plans, and an occasional pilot project. Money is also expended, of course, to develop programs to solicit money to develop more surveys and plans. Pilot programs are usually those that are done through the initiative of other organizations but which are placed by them under the umbrella of the nonprofit banqueteers in hopes of obtaining some of the banqueteers' money for expanding the pilot program.

The banquets are usually blessed with the presence of numerous senators and congressmen who attend primarily because they will be at the table of leading constituents or potential campaign contributors who, in turn, attend primarily because they will be at the table of congressmen and senators.

Five hours, twenty awards, and twenty-four speeches[1] later, the nonprofit organization brings its banquet to a moanistic conclusion, having accomplished nothing but appearing to have accomplished much. The guests quickly leave the banquet hall, and smile as they silently pledge to themselves never to return.

Citizens watching the bureaucrats of nonprofit organizations or any other institution usually have little difficulty in spotting the beginning bureaucrats.

The fledgling bureaucrat, for example, tends to speak in simple terms and may actually answer a question or impart some knowledge. *Professionally mature bureaucrats never speak until they have nothing to say.*

A new bureaucrat might cheerfully move forms and reports around a desk, but an old-timer will appear worried and profoundly concerned as papers are slowly shuffled with thoughtful deliberation. Even citizens who are dedicated bureaucrat-watchers sometimes have difficulty in identifying various categories of apparently mature bureaucrats. The best single test for distinguishing an amateur bureaucrat from a professional bureaucrat in a committee or staff meeting is a simple one: the professional bureaucrat never snores.

Many bureaucratic fledglings accept their work assignments, assuming there are such, with the attitude that there is a job to be done and they are to help do it. Very little time passes, however, before the new employee begins to learn that the operation of rules, procedures, and personnel domains results in a constant reassessment and justification of all aspects of a task.

---

[1] The message of most such speeches appear to be based on the experiences of Spot, Puff, Dick and Jane. See Gray, William S. and Lillian Gray, *Fun with Dick and Jane* (New York: Scott, Foresman and Company, 1947).

The yes-buts, the orbital dialogues, and the decision postponement patterns of bureaucracy begin to have an effect on the enthusiasm of the newcomer. The first stages of *mellownization* may be set into motion.

Mellownization is a life process, and it is related to the ethereal inertness of the status quo that is multigenerational in nature. It is a process that is transmitted from generation to generation and from age to age. Youthful dynamism, and the creative surges that derive from it, are often ground to a halt after continual confrontation with the tough facts of life and the special interests that tend to make the facts tough.

Mellownization, the process of decelerating demands for change and progress, tends to accompany the process of aging, but it is essentially a function of experience, accommodation, and resignation.

As dynamic action is replaced by dynamic inaction, and as the progressive surges are replaced with retrogressive shuffles, a balance is struck between resilient drive and steadfast nesting. An operational status quo is the result.

Bureaucracy, once viewed as being the intricate and rather wasteful functioning of governmental bureaus, is no longer recognized as the private province of public servants alone.[2] Corporations abound with artisans in orbital dialoguing, and the separation of management from ownership gives creative nonresponsiveness to stockholders' interests an opportunity to flourish. Automobile insurance companies can keep legitimate claims in orbit for years before making a settlement; huge conglomerates can develop organizational charts that make even the milicrats[3] of the

[2] See Boren, *When In Doubt, Mumble: A Bureaucrat's Handbook*, (New York: Von Nostrand Reinhold, 1972) for a wadistic commentary on corporate and academic bureaucracy.

[3] *Milicrat* is a term first used by columnist John Cramer of Washington, D.C., to describe the military practitioners of the bureaucratic art.

Pentagon issue sighs of admiration; and academic thrummers, from kindergarten through graduate school, can thrash paper and orchestrate meetings until teaching becomes an incidental part of the educational process.

Even the legislative practitioners (political bureaucrats; polibus [poly-booze]), once the citizens' defenders against bureaucratic inaction or bureaucratic excesses, have begun to accept bureaucracy as an inevitable feature of a mature society.

Legislative mellownization is fostered by the polibus' constant search for comfortable nesting grounds to which they may flutter when political defeat or retirement comes. Few polibus will burn their bridges to possible appointment to positions in the executive branch. Legislative mellownization, therefore, softens the once effective demands for service by governmental agencies—demands that once characterized the legislative "voice of the people."

The muffled sounds from the Congress of the United States, for example, are public denouncements of the White House encroachment upon the powers of the Congress. They are the fortissimo accompaniment of the pianissimo delegation of constitutional authority from and by the Congress to the executive branch. Legislative mellownization may be the final stage in the search for the philosophical status quo.

All great movements have been built upon philosophical foundations, but the cesspoolian growth of the bureaucratic movement, though often described with olfactorical preciseness, has never been articulated in philosophical terms. The essence of bureaucracy can be sensed by citizens throughout the world, but those practicing bureaucrats who are most deeply immersed in its substantive functions cry out for a philosophy of their own.

Chapter 2

A Philosophical Basis for Bureaucracy

The heart, the mind, and the soul of personkind have interactingly moved through the ages with surging tranquility in the intellectual pursuit of nothingness. The bureaucratic way of life, based on maximized nothingness, has a heritage as old and glorious as the first philosophical murmurings to be orchestrated within the human spirit.

Lao-tse, the great philosopher of the sixth century B.C., was concerned with purposeless murmurings, and may be considered the first philosopher to show the inner spirit of our bureaucratic way of life. In the *Tao-Teh-King* are words of inspiring wisdom to bureaucrats:

> A state may be ruled by measures of correction; weapons of war may be used with crafty dexterity; *but the kingdom is made one's own only by freedom from action and purpose.*[1]

Thus, freedom from action and freedom from purpose have been goals long recognized as being keys to mastering kingdoms.

[1] *The Tao-Teh-King*, Part I, Chapter 57, 1. Italics are the author's.

The philosophical murmurings of inaction were also at the heart of the prodigious pondering that excited the ancient Greeks. They preferred intellectual contemplation to the vulgar vagaries of action. Contemplation leading to direct action was contemplation devoutly to be avoided, but contemplation leading to more exciting contemplation was contemplation to be pursued.[2]

While the truths of dynamic inaction and the essences of the bureaucratic movement have been known to bureaucrats through the ages, it is important that the study of inaction and purposelessness be put in proper perspective.

For purposes of philosophical study, therefore, let us establish three levels of *freedom from action and purpose* (acronymistically to be referred to as *FAP*):

    (1) The level of *Greater Freedom from Action and Purpose* (G-FAP);

    (2) The level of *Moderated Freedom from Action and Purpose* (M-FAP);

    (3) The level of *Lesser Freedom from Action and Purpose* (L-FAP).

The G-FAP level is the goal toward which all bureaucrats strive but few actually reach. It is the highest and purest form of inaction and purposelessness, and its attainment opens the doors to the great ballroom of the epicurean bureaucrat.

Some students of bureaucracy view G-FAP as being a philosophical blend of conceptual nothingness and Plato's level of ineffability. G-FAPPERS are most often found at the highest levels of bureaucracies, and if not actually the holders of the highest offices, they

2Author's note: It is hoped that the parametric harmonics of contemplative interfacing has been made quite clear. Excellent resource material can be found in the *Congressional Record* for the first Ninety-Two Congresses of the United States.

may be the Special Assistants or Administrative Assistants that mumblingly flutter around thronistic environs. There are many G-FAPPERS, however, to be found in the middle level of bureaucracies, because bureaucrats can move up the ladder to G-FAPPERY while not necessarily moving up the career ladder in terms of official position.

The L-FAP level involves slightly active inaction and partly purposeful purposelessness. L-FAPPERS are those at the operational levels who strive to become G-FAPPERS and, therefore, must show occasional bursts of activity in order to guide their nests in the direction of G-FAPPERY. Bureaucrats who are concerned with the realities (*sic*) of life must tolerate philosophical impurities in order to pursue the purpose of being purposeless, and they must be active enough to move bureaucratic patterns of behavior toward total inaction.

Moderated Freedom from Action and Purpose (M-FAP) is the level between L-FAP and G-FAP. It is the level of those bureaucrats who have sought to move from L-FAPPERY to G-FAPPERY but have failed for some reason. Perhaps they were unable to recognize G-FAP when they saw it, or perhaps they were too active in their inaction and overshot the target of total purposelessness. Some bureaucrats at the M-FAP level may become tired of constantly directing themselves toward total purposelessness. They may simply give up rather than be devoted fully to maintaining a sufficient level of purposeful purposelessness to attain the G-FAP level of total purposelessness.[3]

[3]M-FAPPERS in the United States who are great moderators in all they do, received great encouragement from observing national programs of moderated honesty and adjustive integrity. Such moderation and adjustivity have long been recognized in Texas politics where the woolen hood of moderation has been employed to reduce the political acuity of the citizens. It has been called party harmony.

From L-FAPPERY to G-FAPPERY

Bureaucrats at the level of Lesser Freedom from Action and Purpose (L-FAP) recognize that goal-oriented activity may undermine their survival foundation, but they also accept the fact that the long-range retrogression of personkind demands the development of protective procedures.

To move backwards to the known may be as dangerous as to move forward to the unknown, but a webbistic pattern of protective procedures is always being woven with the hind leg of bureaucratic forethought. The threads of bureaucratic activity are woven into patterns of behavior that respond to various elements of the environment. It is the response to the external and internal environments that characterizes the crosshatching of bureaucratic procedures.

Students of the philosophy of bureaucracy concern themselves with individual or institutional response by intellect and emotions or mind and body. Some students of the psychology of bureaucracy, however, limit their concern to the response factors of the external and internal environments.

Bureaucrats may be variously affected by the size, location, and status aspects of their respective offices, for example. They may react in different ways to the sounds of typewriters as their secretaries hesitantly type, erase, and opaque an urgent and important memorandum to the White House, agency head, or chairman of the board.

Bureaucrats may respond differently to the same external environment because of different internal environmental factors. One bureaucrat may arrive at the conference table after an excellent breakfast, a warm send-off at home, and a leisurely drive to the office. Another bureaucrat may arrive at the same conference table after burned toast and poor coffee, a shrieking farewell at home, and a fender-scraping race to the office.

If the two bureaucrats are asked their recommendations on the possible actions that their superior should take, the first bureaucrat may handle the question with a cautious response that would harmonize with what he thinks the superior wants to hear. The second bureaucrat, however, may steamingly tell his superior precisely what he might do and where he might go. Successful bureaucrats are those who effectively control the outward response patterns regardless of the churning of the internal spirit.

The move from L-FAPPERY to G-FAPPERY requires the careful orchestration of environmental responses in order that the thought processes may be clearly directed toward developing procedures, forms, and policies. Such procedures, forms, and policies guide colleagues and outsiders into making decisions that result in prodigious pondering and intellectual contemplation.

An L-FAP bureaucrat in a public or private entity may find that there exists in the organization many feasibility studies, studies of studies, and surveys of the reviews of studies of studies. As a special assistant to a senior officer of the organization, the L-FAPPER may work with friends in the personnel office or on the board of directors to obtain a new position as orchestrator of all studies. He will thus have been somewhat active in obtaining the position of orchestrator of studies, which is, of course, the most nothing position in any organization.

When L-FAPPERS do become intermittently active, they make every effort to maintain a low profile and move with great caution. Operational bureaucrats implement programs of moderated nothingness in order to work toward the goal of optimal nothingness.

Intellectual contemplation may be institutionalized into commissions and committees and ultimately may be expressed as general policy goals. Adjustive goals may subsequently lead to guidelines, and guidelines may be further institutionalized into more formal rules and regulations. Rules and regulations may be subjected to periodic reexamination by commissions and committees. Evaluation procedures, of course, give proper consideration to the patterns of behavior that characterize the practitioners of the bureaucratic art, and patterns of behavior are considered in the light of environmental factors. The orbs may ebb but ebbing is always within bureaucratic orbits.

The great orbits of bureaucratic inactivity will continue through the ages and perhaps edge closer and closer to the purity of total inactivity and undeniable purposelessness. It is only through dedicated adherence to the construction of webbistic walls of protective procedures and through the application of the principles of dynamic inaction that L-FAPPERY may ultimately become the G-FAPPERY which philosophers and practitioners of bureaucracy have sought through the ages.

The drive for nonresponsiveness and the missionary cause of dynamic inaction are things of the spirit. The spirit of bureaucracy can be found in the brightness of day and the darkness of night, in the movement from minimal activity to the effervescent excitement of Nirvanic inactivity, and in the trend from the descriptive level of random purposes to the ineffable level of inspiring purposelessness.

"Ah, Bureaucracy!" said the poet, "inaction be thy name; purposelessness be thy game."[4] And of such is the philosophical basis of bureaucracy, for bureaucracy is, indeed, a way of life.

---

[4] From a soliloquy presented by a distinguished philosopher-sculptor-poet at an office picnic of the office of the general counsel of a major federal agency which must be nameless but which deals with veterans' affairs. Johnston-on-Hillside, Harpers Ferry, West Virginia, Summer 1972.

Chapter 3

Behavioral Profile of a Bureaucrat

An understanding of the philosophical base from which bureaucrats operate is important for any serious student of the bureaucratic art. It is the application of the philosophy, however, that gives the average citizen who must work for a living the tonal characteristics that will enable identification of practicing bureaucrats.

Physical identification of a bureaucrat is exciting, but learning something of the behavioral pattern of a bureaucrat opens the door to even greater insights into the species being observed, and in fact, insights into the entire *familia bureaucraticus*. An Ottawa bureaucrat visiting Brasilia or a Washington bureaucrat visiting Moscow will be limited both in knowledge gained and joy attained unless communication can be conducted in the language of the country visited. Patterns of cross-cultural communication cannot be developed without understanding the language being sung, and the philosophy and behavioral elements of a people.

What, then, are the general characteristics of a bureaucrat's life style that will help a taxpayer know a bureaucrat when he sees one? What are the patterns of behavior that can be used as identification guidelines for bureaucrat-watchers?

Observations from a
Bureaucrat-Watcher's Notebook

1. *When in charge, bureaucrats prodigiously ponder.*
They use gestures and facial expressions to indicate
deep thought, total authority, and total concern; and
they do it in a noncommittal way. Amateur bureaucrat-watchers often expect to see the bureaucrat-in-
charge do something, but experienced observers know
that bureaucratic chiefs only ponder and orchestrate.

2. *When in trouble, bureaucrats delegate.* When
trouble appears on the horizon, experienced bureaucrats
immediately delegate all responsibilities that have the
slightest relationship to whatever trouble may possibly
develop. Inexperienced delegators tend to shuffle fran-
tically when they delegate, but those that have with-
stood the storms of crises past, handle delegating situations with such deftness that those to whom the
impending trouble has been delegated do not realize
it until it is too late.

3. *When in doubt, bureaucrats mumble.* This is the
basic watchword of all experienced bureaucrats in all
classes of bureaucracies. When the mumbler mumbles
with eloquence, few citizens will challenge either the
thrust of the mumbled message or the rationale of
the thrust, whatever the listener guesses it to be.

Mumbling is an age-old art form that is used by
people in all walks of life, and it is particularly useful
to bureaucrats or nonbureaucrats alike when they do
not wish to be quoted. A mumble and a smile can
never be quoted.

4. *Bureaucrats never speak their minds. To even
suggest such a thing would be devoid of wisdom.* The
professional bureaucrat never reveals the vacuity of
his thought processes. To do so would threaten status
and security.

The flush of ideas in a bureaucratic mind is like the
flush of a toilet. The ideas are usually past their prime

16

and better expelled than retained. The primary expelling process is sometimes referred to as mumbling, and it involves the projection of minimal thought patterns.

5. *Bureaucrats never say simply what they can say professionally.* From time to time, the devoted bureaucrat-watcher will sight a group of bureaucrats as they discover a new and simple project. With unrestrained joy, they tear into the new project, and immediately profundicate or profundify it.[1]

The joy of profundification is the inner force that converts many practicing bureaucrats into missionaries for the movement. (Missionary-oriented bureaucrats are constantly seeking simple ideas to convert.) Profundification is related to vertical mumbling, but it goes beyond verbal communication.

Vertical mumbling is characterized by tonal intelligibility with admixturized overtones of translocated syllables. Vertical mumblers are the most skilled of all mumblers, and they are capable of stringing multisyllabattic words with quantitized extension.[2] Mumbling with verticality permits professional bureaucrats to communicate with one another while communicating with no one else; mumbling is the international language of bureaucracy.

Profundification is the bureaucratic skill of interfacing patterns of vertical mumbling with principles of con-

---

[1] *To profundify* and *to profundicate* are bureaucratic verbs that mean the same thing. Graduates of the Ivy League schools tend to use *profundify* while graduates of state universities and agricultural colleges tend to use *profundicate*. Thus, profundication = profundification; profundicator = profundifier. Bureaucrat-watchers should recognize that the difference is not one of meaning or depth but of origin.

[2] The Pentagon, The State Department, and the Department of Housing and Urban Development are the graduate schools of the mumblistic arts, but the White House has made great strides in mumbling inoperability in recent years. For those wishing to learn how to mumble vertically or linearly, see Boren, *When In Doubt, Mumble.*

ceptual celibacy. The blend is foggistic artistry at its best. Senior level bureaucrats must be profundicators; it is an unwritten part of their job description. Middle level bureaucrats use the term and apply the principles of obscuration, but no self-respecting bureaucrat likes to obscurate when they can develop the higher skill of profundification. Many of the governmental, academic, and corporate programs of internships have been developed to teach the principles of profundification to aspiring bureaucrats.

It is not possible to identify profundicating bureaucrats by their plumage or nesting habits; they can be identified only by carefully reading their tracks or listening to their songs.

6. *If a bureaucrat mumbles long enough, people will begin to think he is making sense.*[3] Short-term mumblers fail, but marathon mumblers usually gain the reputation of being experts.

7. *Marginal thoughts that are mumbled with enthusiasm can prevail over logical arguments that are articulated with solemnity and clarity.* Enthusiasm and direct eye-to-eye contact are more effective than logic, because people can understand enthusiasm and eyeballing easier than they can understand logic. Many bureaucrats combine enthusiasm and eye contact and smiles as they mumble their never-to-be-remembered messages. If it is worth saying, it is worth mumbling!

8. *Bureaucrats are the only people in the world who can say absolutely nothing and mean it.* Citizens normally believe that communication requires something

[3]The use of the personal pronoun *he* does not necessarily reflect that the author is a male chauvinist. It does reflect, however, the author's view that women make poor bureaucrats. They tend to want answers to their questions; they move directly to resolve problems; and they rarely mumble. There is hope for the future, however, because an increasing number of women in the banking and personnel fields are beginning to adopt the bureaucratic way of life.

to be communicated, but bureaucrats never speak until they have nothing to say. In fact, there appears to be a very basic rule that bureaucrats follow in the matter of verbal communications; *If you can't say more than you know, don't say it.*

Highly placed bureaucrats in the White House during the Nixon Administration learned the lesson well when they made the mistake of saying less than they knew. Had they followed the bureaucratic rule, and said more than they knew, the credibility of misspeaking might have been established, and historical inoperability might have been accepted. To say more than one knows, of course, is to say nothing, and that is the true spirit of orbital dialoguing.

9. *Corporate bureaucrats are artisans in publicly blasting the governmental bureaucracy they are privately copying.* The corporate bureaucrats have gone far beyond the governmental bureaucrats in: (1) organizational patterns; (2) responsiveness to their constituencies; and (3) ability to keep secrets.

The United States Government has only one vice president, for example, and at times may have great difficulty in obtaining the one. The corporate bureaucracy, on the other hand, is filled to overflowing with vice presidents. One major transportation company has 108 of them. There are functional vice presidents that actually function, but there are many functional vice presidents that simply hover around the executive offices. Hovering is facilitated, of course, by: (1) the complexity of the organizational charts, and (2) the separation of management from ownership in corporate operations.

10. *The ego of many beginning bureaucrats drives them to seek pedestals on which they can climb. Old-timers know better.* Pedestals make for better targets, and experienced bureaucrats prefer to residuate (maintain a low profile) except in rare and carefully selected

instances. If a citizen sees a fully-grown man or woman on a pedestal, it can be assumed that either a non-bureaucrat is in view, or that despite the level of physical maturity, the specimen is a beginning bureaucrat.

Taxpayers should remember that mayors, governors, and presidents occasionally appoint to public positions fully mature persons from the business, labor, academic, or professional worlds. Beginning bureaucrats who are physically mature are often more fun to watch than beginning bureaucrats who are of the younger or puffed fledgling category.

11. *Innovative bureaucrats, like whooping cranes, are rare birds, and their thought projections can have dangerous impact. Bureaucratic thoughts on earth are like weightlessness in space; unattached policies may float with ease until they catch some taxpayer in the neck.* Bureaucrat-watchers, therefore, should exercise caution when in the vicinity of a group of feeding or nesting bureaucrats. When bureaucrats know that they are being watched, they may begin mumbling and casting forth unattached policies and nondirective directives. It can be dangerous.

12. *There is no such thing as a virginal bureaucrat. Bureaucratic virgins there may be, but virginal bureaucrats there will never be.* The very birth process of bureaucrats precludes it because the process involves the motherhood of citizens and the fatherhood of bureaucrats. Experienced bureaucrat-watchers have noted that people are finally admitted to the personhood of bureaucracy when they have actually completed what is known as the institutional transaction with a citizen. All citizens ultimately learn that the impregnable forces of governmental, corporate, academic, and religious bureaucracies have impinged upon their lives in some manner.

Many corporate bureaucrats of the oil industry, for example, were admitted to the personhood of bureaucracy during the energy crisis as they gave service to the consuming public. Automobile insurance companies have qualified many of their corporate employees for membership in the personhood as they applied the principles of creative nonresponsiveness to the insurance claims of their clients in all states or provinces and in all rural areas where they operate. Many academic thrummers have attained bureaucratic sainthood as they guided the inquiring spirit of students into the safer waters of becalmed puerility.

Citizens of all nations and in all walks of life know that the creativity of bureaucracy lies in the constant search by bureaucrats to find new ways of doing the same old thing to the public and to one another that they have always done through the ages. Herein lies the drama of one-upmanship and the spirit of bureaucratic deblahsification.

13. *The Boren Principle of Error Implementation:* Errors implemented by inaction are less dangerous than errors implemented by action. Errors by inaction have less impact and more mushistic graduality than errors of action. Graduality provides time for adjustment and accommodation, and permits institutional homeostasis to take place. The degree of graduality is the Mush Factor of Error Implementation.

Chapter 4

Habitats

Bureaucrats come in all shapes and sizes, and they are to be found wherever people live, work, or play. There is, in fact, a touch of the bureaucrat in everyone, and few, if any, endeavors are untouched by bureaucratic principles and the red tape that binds.

The Thursday Morning Study Club has its committees and procedures that are strikingly similar to the committees and procedures of the United Nations. The constitution and by-laws of the teachers' organization in Calgary, Alberta, is very similar to those of the teachers' organizations in Austin, Texas, and Montego Bay, Jamaica.

The chambers of commerce, parent teachers associations, recreation clubs, civic clubs, and churches are institutions that propose resolutions blasting governmental bureaucracy and, then, send copies of the proposed resolutions to their committee chairmen for clearance and routing to the committee members, subcommittee members, and other interested parties.

The habitats of bureaucrats are everywhere. The spirit of creative nonresponsiveness and dynamic inaction knows no bounds.

Like most other members of the animal kingdom, bureaucrats like to travel, and many of their shufflistic movements are directed to obtaining travel orders so that they can fly away from the headquarters nest from time to time. Such migrations are usually of short duration, but they enable the L-FAPPERS and M-FAPPERS, described in Chapter 2, to range afield under the guise of experts. Governmental bureaucrats arrange migratory flights as inspection trips or TDY; academic bureaucrats wrap their flight plans in the fabric of professional conferences; and corporate bureaucrats speak of business trips, whether they be sales meetings, conventions, or lobbying efforts.

Though bureaucrats can be found everywhere, they tend to hover near their nests, and bureaucrat-watchers can find particular joy in observing nesting sites.

Bureaucrats in the Home

Mother bureaucrats are the first teachers of things bureaucratic. A newborn infant is barely placed in its mother's arms before becoming the target of soft cooistic mumblings. Fathers, other relatives, neighbors, and total strangers all contribute to the mumblings until the baby reaches the awkward age of later infancy. At that time, the cooisms give way to directory orders that may be punctuated by digital and rumperatory slaps. The child soon learns in the home that lesson which it will learn again in later years: do what told to do, without regard to what superiors do themselves.

Mother bureaucrats not only teach their young the eternal verities of bureaucracy but they also serve as teachers who instruct their mates in the importance of nest-feathering and gift-bearing. Mother bureaucrats, of course, orchestrate the nocturnal schedules in the nest by low-key singing of tiredness and headaches.

Father bureaucrats once taught their young the

principles of baseball, basketball, and football during exercise periods in the nesting area, but such principles are now taught by hurried conversations during television commercials. Instruction in sports is a vital element of early training for future bureaucrats, because it stresses the importance of the good of the team. Active participation in sports and inactive participation in religious services are essential steps in teaching the young the importance of institutionalizing patterns of behavior.

During the adolescent period, youthful apprentices learn the importance of appropriate clearances. On questions of evening hours, mother bureaucrats give the clearance; on questions of trips for sporting events, father bureaucrats give the clearance; and on the use of the family car, appeals from mother's decisions are taken to father bureaucrat—but with a wary eye on the former. Few appeals are made from father bureaucrats to mother bureaucrats, because the young beginners soon learn to avoid the irrevocable-once-given negative answer from the theoretical head of the nest. Fledglings soon learn an important lesson: better avoided than tested.

Though father bureaucrats are the titular heads of nests, most job descriptions in household bureaucracies are written by mother bureaucrats. As Wilma Cheek, a noted philosopher of the bridge table, once observed: "Roosting roosters would rather roost with tranquil acceptance of daily domination than be doomed to an eternity of tiredness and headaches." Her husband did not disagree.

Bureaucracies in the home, therefore, tend to be matriarchal in nature. Their primary function is to produce and train fledglings that can transmit the bureaucratic heritage to future generations when they become chief hoverers of their own nests.

Bureaucrats in the Church

Churches, as institutions, are the natural spiritual residences for solemn bureaucracy. Though religious institutions deal with the substance of joy, they tend to express the joyousness of their being in gloomy invitations, heavy-hearted threats, and solemn rituals. The inner joy and outward solemnity of religious expression constitute a pattern of behavioral communication that gives comfort to nonsectarian as well as sectarian bureaucrats.

All religious societies have two basic kingdoms in which they operate: (1) administration from Above; and, (2) procedural rituals.

Though bureaucracy is widely known as the world's second oldest profession, the philosophers and historians of the bureaucratic movement quietly admit that the scrolls and chards of yesteryear indicate that bureaucracy emerged: (1) as the world's oldest profession was being institutionalized, and (2) as the prophets were establishing channels of communication through the exchange of informal scrolls, memoranda, and newsletters. Regardless of the origins, however, the historical facts speak with clarion gravity. Religion and bureaucracy have walked the same organizational paths since the beginning of recorded history.

Institutionalization, of course, requires organization. Organization, in turn, cannot be accomplished as a preliminary to institutionalization without a plan for administration, and administration certainly requires organizational charts. One of the highest art forms that flourished during the early religious expansionist movement was that of organogramming or chart-making.[1]

[1] The critics of bureaucratic art have long bemoaned the disappearance of classical organization charts whose dignity is in sharp contrast to the lines and boxes that are drawn today with artistic minimality.

25

Great organizational charts helped to point the way to build magnificent administrative structures that could stimulate the development of not only immediate religious institutions but also of related foundations, private enterprises, and public bingo.

Reflected in the organizational charts have been the governing boards of the religious societies. Each religious group, of course, has developed its own system of government, complete with executive, legislative, and judicial functions. Operating under various names and functioning with different degrees of power, the governing boards receive nominations for titles and position. From such nominations, they select the supernal authorities. The chief administrator, on earth, for each of the religious organizations approximates the "administration from Above" as close as an earthly "Above" can be approximated. ("Administration from Above" is known simply as *the AA* in some parts of the United States and Canada.)

Bureaucrat-watchers have made many studies of the parallel development of the AA in religious and political organizations. Apart from the housekeeping function of religious institutions are the vital rituals that are at the heart of many religious movements.

As seasoned bureaucrat-watchers will testify, all bureaucrats recognize the sanctity of established channels and procedures. In no other place is this more evident than in the conduct of various religious rites. Under the threat of extreme penalties, practicing bureaucrats rigidly adhere to the letter of procedural rituals even though the ceremonial intonations may be mumbled linearly.

Linear mumblers tend to be found at the bottom of religious hierarchies as they are in other hierarchies. Vertical mumblers are the superior mumblers.

Teachers, clergymen, and bureaucrats are the most proficient vertical mumblers in the world. If a person

26

happens to be all three at once, the heavens of ineffability shall be opened, and the marginal wisdom of the ages shall be proclaimed with convincing resonance! *Such is the Trinity of Bureaucracy.* (Lawyers, of course, are not included in the bureaucratic trinity because they are in a hypostatic class by themselves.) All secular bureaucrats regularly pay homage to the leaders of religious organizations for the outstanding manner in which they have institutionalized the survival process.

Bureaucrat-watchers can find no richer environ for observing bureaucrats at work and play than can be found in the churchyards of the world.

Corporate Bureaucracy

Corporate bureaucrats have publicly declared war on the red tape and excessive procedures of governmental bureaucrats. While waging the public war against bureaucracy, the corporate leaders have privately used most of the management mechanisms they have criticized. In matters of organization, the corporate bureaucrats have often led the way for governmental practitioners.

One airline in the United States, for example, lists 108 vice presidents. Another airline has developed an organizational chart that appropriately shows the relationships and duties of its executives in a huge circle. The executives appear to move in a wide orbit with fuzzified lines of authority implied but not defined.

Administration by committee has also become a well-accepted vehicle through which responsibility can be shifted in a nondirective manner and through which decisions can be postponed while having the appearance of sound management.

A number of professional bureaucrats (and a few political leaders) have envied the corporate world and its successfully fuzzified principles of administration. More particularly, however, the number of vice presidents that corporations can orbit is viewed with sparkling jealousy. With the United States Government having only one vice president for ceremonial and other minor purposes, the governmental bureaucrats feel somewhat inferior institutionally.

Corporate bureaucracies provide excellent opportunities for observing bureaucratic life styles. Personnel offices, governmental relations offices, public affairs offices, legal offices, offices of comptrollers and budgeteers, and other nonline offices are noted nesting areas for corporate bureaucrats. Few genuine bureaucrats will be found in the sales or production lines of corporate bureaucracies, because they are too busy working to support the rest of the corporate structure by doing whatever it was that the corporation was established to do.[2] The production and sales people do not have time to diddle, daddle, or doodle. They are poor bureaucrats.

Academic Bureaucracies

With the possible single exception of automobile insurance companies, there is no bureaucracy like the bureaucracy of an educational institution. Administrators overadminister, and teachers underteach. Many casual observers of acabus (academic bureaucrats) think that teachers spend their time in classrooms teaching students and introducing them to the thrill of learning. Experienced observers of acabus, however, know that teachers usually assign busy-work to their students in order that they can fill out the forms and make the reports required by the administrators of the school system, the county offices, state authorities, various federal agencies, and the PTA. When not occupied filling out these forms, teachers can then give

[2]For related reading on non-diddle-daddle-doodlers, see Alger, Horatio, Jr., *Struggling Upward* (New York: Hurst & Company, undated).

their attention to other priorities such as fund-raising campaigns, NEA or AFT questionnaires, and coordinate announcements about the sporting events, school plays band concerts, observances for Save-the-Cockroaches Week, and plans for the school trip to city hall.

Bureaucrat-watchers, therefore, can find bureaucracy at work and bureaucrats at frustrated play at almost any time of the day, but bureaucrat-watchers in the land of academe may some day find teachers doing something that they have never observed before. They should take very careful note, because they may be observing a teacher teaching!

Other Habitats

Merely to list the habitats of bureaucrats would be to compile the yellow pages of the telephone books from every city and village of the world.

Civic clubs abound with committees, forms, and ritual; neighborhood associations develop guidelines for swimming contests and standards of measurement for avenue potholes. Adjusters for automobile insurance companies are masters in orchestrating the postponement patterns on clients' claims; city bus companies can switch locations of bus stops with the same ease that the Internal Revenue Service changes its income tax forms each year.

College admission officers can keep prospective students swinging slowly in midair almost as long as it takes a critically ill patient on a stretcher to complete the forms for admission to a hospital. A thirty-minute newscast on radio or television evolves from a frantic shuffling of paper and sifting of notes.

The housewife who dialogues with the sanitation department on garbage pick-up and the man who hassles with automobile agencies over warranty service know that bureaucrats can be found behind garbage cans or under the hoods of cars.

29

And as one ponders the limitless range of bureaucrats, flights of fantasy come crashing to earth when one inquiringly wonders what bureaucratic patterns must exist in a colony of ants, a swarm of bees, or a gaggle of geese. 'Tis gaggling devoutly to be wished.

Part II

THE BUREAUCRAT-WATCHER'S MANUAL

(An Introduction to Ornibureaucratology)

One need not be an ornithologist to reap great pleasure from bird-watching. With powerful glasses in hand, a bird-watcher's manual in pocket, and an inquiring spirit of mind and heart, many people have found excitement in observing birds at work and birds at play. There are birds that are large, and there are birds that are small. There are birds that are relatively quiet, and there are birds that are noisy. There are country birds that feed upon the seeds of the field and the fruits of the orchards, and there are city birds that feed upon the refuse of personkind. Though deep knowledge of birds is not necessary to enjoy watching them, an understanding of the life cycle, the habitat, the feeding habits, and the patterns of behavior add to the thrill of rare or even frequent sightings of different species of birds.

Similarly, the joy of

bureaucrat-watching is enhanced not only by recognizing physical profiles but also by understanding the essence of bureaucracy, the work and play habits of bureaucrats, and the techniques of moving bureaucrats from one roosting position to another.

No species of bureaucrat has ever become extinct, but new ones evolve from the random interfacing of bureaucrats and taxpayers. The progression of bureaucracy is endless and ageless, but new discoveries and new insights into the life styles of developing bureaucrats can be helpful to private citizens who may be preparing to do battle with the forces of bureaucracy.

Or, perhaps recollections of old insights will enable bureaucrat-watchers to relax in some corner of the great aviary and simply enjoy the farcicalities of the bureaucrats as they flutter, hover, and cover.

It is in this spirit that *Part II* is presented as the bureaucrat-watcher's constant companion.

Chapter 5

GENUS
Nesting Sinecurists

A genus of bureaucrats
who don't know what to do,
don't care,
and don't do anything.

☞ Yesbutting Negates

- BEHAVIORAL PATTERNS: This species of bureaucrat rarely leaves the nest, but members of the species can be observed from time to time raising their heads above the nest to interject their call into discussions on policy or day-to-day operations. Policy makers or program managers are well acquainted with the shrill call of the species. Being scavengers, the Yesbutting Negates will eat and drink anything as long as it is free.
- PROFILES AND PLUMAGE: Questioning profile; wild plumage.
- HABITAT: Usually found resting in nests located in corporate, academic, religious, and governmental bureaucracies. Found at all levels.
- CALL: Shrill call echoes in conference rooms and through marble halls: "Yes, but . . . y-e-s, but. . . ."

Obsequious Negates

- BEHAVIORAL PATTERNS: Related to the Yesbutting Negates, the Obsequious Negates are easily recognized as nonthinkers who, when frightened at the prospect of having to make a decision on their own, hide behind *the regulations*. This species is a slow mover that shifts with Peteristic surety from one level of incompetence to another. (The Peter Principle never really applies in its purest sense, because Obsequious Negates never *reach* their level of incompetence. They start there.)
- PROFILES AND PLUMAGE: Head bowed or ducked, hands folded with constant fingerflexing. Plumage is trampled.
- HABITAT: Found in all bureaucracies, but most common in the lower and middle branches of governmental structures.
- CALL: Obsequious Negates sing with unctuatory softness and sympathetic syrupdippity as they explain why something can't be done or a decision can't be made. "Look, if it were up to me . . .; But you have the wrong form . . .; I wish I could help, but the regulations say. . . ."

35

Conference Doodlers

- BEHAVIORAL PATTERNS: Members of this species range short distances from their nests to roost quietly at conference tables. Noted for surrealistic doodling, Conference Doodlers tend to focus their eyes on doodles-in-process. They occasionally cast a questioning look at conference dialoguers and may slightly nod their heads. Some of the species, at the conclusion of conferences, tilt their heads slightly to one side, slowly raise their heads, and move their beak in an arc; this pattern of behavior projects a silent message of contempt through half-closed eyes. Conference Doodlers do nothing but doodle, but they doodle well.
- PROFILES AND PLUMAGE: Head downward over conference tables, arms encircling doodling paper, elbows on table. Plumage, tired.
- HABITAT: All bureaucracies. Many bridge players provide opportunities for doodling by distributing multiple copies of score pads.
- CALL: Some Conference Doodlers emit a series of low volume sounds by popping their tongues at the roof of the mouth, while others may be simple cluckers.

- BEHAVIORAL PATTERNS: Intellectual Virgins rarely leave their first nesting places and thrive on food regurgitated by elders. They thrive particularly well in corporate nests, but do quite well in academic and governmental environs. Often strike a fingertapping pose and appear to be prodigiously pondering the subjects under discussion while actually trying to determine what the subjects are.
- PROFILES AND PLUMAGE: Pearish profile. Heavy plumage on head but tailfeathers are worn from constant nesting.
- HABITAT: All bureaucracies, but most commonly found in the highest branches of corporate bureaucracies. Knowledge of literary works limited to those works that are shown at neighborhood theaters, thus hovering about movie theaters from time to time.
- CALL: "Very interesting. . . ."

☞ Intellectual Virgins

Red-Eyed Olive Divers

Vago de los Ríos

- BEHAVIORAL PATTERNS: An afternoon species. Experts in retrieving olives from ice-bearing and non-ice-bearing glasses. Preciseness in diving tends to falter in successive dives, reflecting possible low fatigue factor. Males and females are equal divers.
- PROFILES AND PLUMAGE: Sagging; frazzled.
- HABITAT: Near-office oases and restaurants. Occasionally leave the darkened and protective oases to peer squintingly at the bright world of reality, but hastily retreat from the blinding problem-world to the security of the oases and their specialized olive groves.
- CALL: "Triple."

Vago de los Ríos

Redbeaked Thrushes

- BEHAVIORAL PATTERNS: An afternoon species related to the Red-Eyed Olive Divers. Gargles and swallows various tinctures throughout most periods of observation. Uses mouth spray before fluttering to home nest.
- PROFILES AND PLUMAGE: Pottistic profile; feathers disarranged; auburn beak that matches eyes and neck feathers.
- HABITAT: Found in oases and offices of all bureaucracies.
- CALL: Sings in loud but raspy voice: "Nawsho mush ice."

- BEHAVIORAL PATTERNS: An afternoon species. Males are very similar in appearance to the Redbeaked Thrush. Females rarely leave their nests.
- PROFILES AND PLUMAGE: Nodding profile; plumage variable.
- HABITAT: Males are often found in company of bright-eyed females in environs of music recitals, concert halls, and Shakespearean theaters. Females usually nesting. All bureaucracies.
- CALL: Very rare utterances are characterized by low key, indistinguishable tonal patterns. Usually nod and slowly move eyelids instead of singing.

☞ Pickled Thrummers

Vago de los Ríos

- BEHAVIORAL PATTERNS: Tend to consort with Pickled Thrummers and Red-Eyed Olive Divers. Mellow Larks always are congenial and love to be loved by all. They readily echo the views last presented in any conference or committee session. Nonperformers but do it pleasantly.
- PROFILES AND PLUMAGE: Classified profile; wandering plumage.
- HABITAT: Found in corporate, governmental, and academic bureaucracies. Normally at the middle branches.
- CALL: "Thash right."

 Mellow Larks

👉 Fluttering Evacuators

- BEHAVIORAL PATTERNS: A late afternoon species. Very similar in clockwatching habits of the Zippy Homing Pigeon, but the flight patterns usually include stops at watering holes and other friendly sites before arrival at home nests. Known in Canada as the *Ottawaian Wahwahs*.
- PROFILES AND PLUMAGE: Profile, leaning; plumage, oiled.
- HABITAT: Found almost exclusively in corporate and governmental nests, but advertising, broadcasting, and publishing corporations provide particularly colorful members of the species.
- CALL: "A quickie. . . ."

 Zippy
Homing Pigeon

- BEHAVIORAL PATTERNS: A late afternoon species. Clockwatchers who are poised for immediate flight at close of business. Always carry attaché cases between home and office, and open them from time to time to update changes in letterheads and telephone booklets. Flying pattern is swift and unerringly toward home. If the driver of a car pool, the Zippy Homing Pigeon often leaves tardy riders.
- PROFILES AND PLUMAGE: Ready.
- HABITAT: Most often found in corporate and governmental nests.
- CALL: "Now!"

Chapter 6

GENUS
Bugling Flaques

A genus of bureaucrats
who don't know what to do,
don't know how to do it,
but know how to put it all into words.

 # Distributing Flaques

- BEHAVIORAL PATTERNS: A special category due to a strange but well-defined metamorphosis that converts newsmen into handout artists who rewrite technical reports and nonmessage speeches. Artistic expression is through the use of mailing plates and press release racks. Extended exposure to flaquistic institutionalization sometimes singes sensitive wings, and the metamorphosis is reversed. Distributing Flaques flaque well when they flaque.
- PROFILES AND PLUMAGE: Embarrassingly sad profile. Variable plumage.
- HABITAT: Though a few are found in academic bureaucracies as special assistants to presidents and chancellors of universities, most of the species are to be found around the executive offices of corporations and governmental agencies. Also common in the offices of elected officials at all levels.
- CALL: "It was announced today. . . ."

Vago de los Rios

👉 Sniping Flycatchers

- BEHAVIORAL PATTERNS: Most of the species have had training and experience as auditors, internal revenue service agents, lawyers, editors, members of dissertation committees, or traffic officers. Proficient in cutting and blue lining the work of others, but never produce original works.
- PROFILES AND PLUMAGE: Pecking profile; unpatterned plumage.
- HABITAT: Found everywhere. Apprentices, however, may be sighted primarily in city halls and state capitols.
- CALL: "Uh oh. . . ."

Vago de los Ríos

👉 Profundicating Wordsmiths

- BEHAVIORAL PATTERNS: Outstanding authorities in stating simple concepts in complicated terms but work quietly behind the scenes as opposed to the Crusty-Feathered Profundicators who work publicly and with other materials. Often assigned to work with committees that produce annual reports of corporations, draft budget messages, and develop management objectives for other speechwriters. Masters of thesauric enrichment, writers of governmental regulations, and designers of forms.
- PROFILES AND PLUMAGE: Tired.
- HABITAT: Found in all bureaucracies, including religious institutions. Offices of Profundicating Wordsmiths are usually small, crowded, and filled with paper.
- CALL: "What's the deadline?"

48

- BEHAVIORAL PATTERNS: The highest developed species of Genus Bugling Flaques. Flying under the umbrella of public relations expertise, both males and females strut in rarified atmospheres, affect the latest styling of plumage, partake of the most expensive grains, and keep abreast of the swingiest language. Some Catbirds spend time and clients' money while impressing other Catbirds.
- PROFILES AND PLUMAGE: Maximized.
- HABITAT: Found in plush offices, elegant suites, and expensive restaurants with credit cards of clients.
- CALL: "On the rocks?"

Strutting Catbirds

Vago de los Rios

🖝 Swallowtailed Touters

- BEHAVIORAL PATTERNS: Very similar in objectives and techniques to the Highflying Puffers, but the pattern is more formal and in different environs. Always seeking to tout The Boss but with *important people* instead of the people of the media.
- PROFILES AND PLUMAGE: Expensive.
- HABITAT: High-level formal receptions, cocktail parties, and fund-raising dinners. Political staff people and the officials of the U.S. Pentagon, State Department, and Postal Corporation* are among the most skillful and prolific Swallowtailed Touters. Flapping unsuccessfully at the edge of the nest may be found the functionaries of the telephone companies, but they haven't quite made it yet.
- CALL: "Yes, The Boss was commenting on that yesterday. . . ."

*The U.S. Postal *Corporation* was once known as the U.S. Postal *Service*. The Corporation is characterized by administrative corpulence, and it now rations the service that the Service once gave.

50

Vago de los Ríos

👉 Highflying Puffers

- BEHAVIORAL PATTERNS: Highflying Puffers are normally sighted during sessions of multiphonic honking as they seek favorable mention of The Boss. They have unlimited expense accounts which are used to purchase food and elixir for the working-birds of the media. (Highflying Puffers can be sighted once or twice a year when they moult their way through periods of depression. During such periods, they are sometimes known as Deflated Truthbirds. When the Truthbirds revert to Puffers, they fearfully probe to learn the songs they sang as Truthbirds.)
- PROFILES AND PLUMAGE: Honking profile; wind-blown plumage.
- HABITAT: Around the media birds.
- CALL: Often pound tables and sing loud and constant arias about the favorable attributes, real or imagined, of The Boss. Sometimes whistle or hum as they count column inches.

Chapter 7

GENUS
Frittering Birdbrains

A genus of bureaucrats
who don't know what to do,
don't care,
and do what comes naturally.

☞ Streaking Jaybirds

Vago de los Ríos

- BEHAVIORAL PATTERNS: Fleet-footed fledglings hope to be seen; waddlistic oldsters hope to be caught. The mamabirds of Streaking Jaybirds, like the mamabirds of Doodlers who doodle them, are sometimes embarrassed by the naturalness of the profiles of the members of the species. Streaking Jaybirds do not always have a well-defined reason for their streaking, but they are intrigued by spaces in and around crowds. Fledglings pant from unusual exertion; oldsters pant from eager anticipation.
- PROFILES AND PLUMAGE: Nude profile; plumage plucked.
- HABITAT: Streaking Jaybirds streak through all types of bureaucracies except those within the Arctic and Antarctic Circles.
- CALL: (Puff!)

👉 Thrusty Payroll Hens

- BEHAVIORAL PATTERNS: Qualified nonspellers and typical nontypers. When in the presence of males of any species, the Thrusty Payroll Hens roll their eyes in helpless wonderment, walk with rumperatory abandon, and often thrust themselves into conversations. Thrusty Payroll Roosters have never been sighted. Some leading orni-bureaucratologists believe that the hens respond to the mating dances of males of all species as long as the dancer appears to be well intentioned and well heeled. Working-birds in the same nesting area view Thrusty Payroll Hens as unnecessary office clutter, but male supervisors of nesting areas believe that the hens improve the nesting environs.
- PROFILES AND PLUMAGE: Profiles are maximized; plumage puffed. Head feathers glisten and are plasticized with a durable spray.
- HABITAT: All types of offices in all types of bureaucracies. Most often found in offices of public relations executives.
- CALL: No audible call; sing their songs through appropriate body language.

Passportive Visabirds

- BEHAVIORAL PATTERNS: Passportive Visabirds measure passport photographs with precision instruments to assure the preciseness of the white margins, and they deal with other vital procedural absolutes. The species are great wielders of rubber stamps and outstanding orchestrators of delay. Properly inspired, a Passportive Visabird can delay papers for many months.
- PROFILES AND PLUMAGE: A few specimens have been seen smiling, but most wear authoritative scowls. Haughty demeanor; variable plumage. Passportive Visabirds of all nations are outstanding masters of the art of haughticality.*
- HABITAT: Found in embassies around the world.
- CALL: "Come back next month. . . ."

*The U.S. Embassy in Kingston, Jamaica, has served as the model for fledgling Visabirds who must learn hautical handling of visa applicants. Presiding Passportive Visabirds keep visa applicants standing in long lines for long periods of time, thus providing optimal opportunity for the sidewalk standees to enjoy alternate periods of sun and rain.

Vago de los Ríos

🖐 Antiseptic Medithrashers

- BEHAVIORAL PATTERNS: Antiseptic Medithrashers are the compilers of files and builders of records. Their frantic thrashing and insistent shrieks can prevent even emergency cases from circumventing the paperwork that must be done for the administrative offices before the first thermometer is jammed or the first needle is shoved. The existence of previous or current records cannot keep the devoted Medithrasher from placing paperwork into the number one priority classification. Both males and females fritter and flutter to assure that the primary function of hospitals will be to compile files and build records. Their emotions are antiseptic.
- PROFILES AND PLUMAGE: Frittering profile; plumage disarranged.
- HABITAT: Usually found in hospital emergency rooms, hospital admitting offices, and doctors' offices; also found in health rooms of educational institutions and some social security offices.
- CALL: "Where were you born. . . . ? Insurance number?"

57

- BEHAVIORAL PATTERNS: Self-preening with nesting exercises. Older female bureaucrats of this species tend to develop a settling profile . . . with outward appearance of productive activity. Very rarely stray far from the nest.
- PROFILES AND PLUMAGE: In outward appearance very similar to the members of Genus Nesting Sinecurists. Outgoing profile; overworked plumage. Eyebrows relocated by plucking and painting.
- HABITAT: Found in all bureaucracies.
- CALL: "But my typewriter's broken. . . ."

👉 Preening Setters

Vago de los Rios

Chapter 8

GENUS
Fleet-Footed Perennials

A genus of bureaucrats
who don't know what to do,
don't care,
and do only what has to be done to survive.

Orbital Fingerpointers

- BEHAVIORAL PATTERNS: When a work assignment is cast before the flock, the clucking sounds that are characteristic of the species become louder but intermittent. Each member of the flock, in sequence, transfers the assignment to the next member by pointing with an index finger or a thumb. Some transfers are accomplished by a slight nod of the head. The process of serially transferring responsibilities to others is known as *the orbital buck*. When an effort is made to fix responsibility for an error, the fingerpointing becomes more vigorous, the orbital buck accelerates, and the clucking is continuing and loud.
- PROFILES AND PLUMAGE: Profiles only as necessary; plumage variable.
- HABITAT: Though usually found in small flocks, the orbital fingerpointers can be found everywhere . . . from the home to the courthouse to the White House. Corporate and governmental bureaucracies abound in the species.
- CALL: Audible but simple clucking. Always accompanied by the jerking motion of finger, thumb, or head.

- BEHAVIORAL PATTERNS: Most sightings occur during periods of management belt-tightening or "reduction in force" (RIF) activities. Frenetic Slotseekers move with hummingbird swiftness from office to office in search of new nesting grounds. When Slotseekers are not seeking slots, however, they are not frenetic but are effective practitioners of bureaucratic residuation.
- PROFILES AND PLUMAGE: Profiles pottish; plumage conservative.
- HABITAT: Found in all types of bureaucracies, but only identifiable during management crisis periods. May be seen in the legislative halls from time to time where they maintain their insuring contacts.
- CALL: "I've always been impressed with the work of your office. . . ."

 Frenetic
Slotseekers

Vago de los Rios

👉 Echosulting Peacocks

- BEHAVIORAL PATTERNS: Best known for the ability to echo sounds of previously popular tunes in the same rhythm and significance but with minor changes in tone. They sing words that clients already know but want to hear again to verify what they already know. Echosulting Peacocks are employed at high rates by management level officials in order to gain support for weak positions.
- PROFILES AND PLUMAGE: Profiles, cautious; plumage, expensive.
- HABITAT: Often found in the same feeding grounds as the Fringeful Hoverers; always within earshot of seats of power. Noted for authoritative strutting in prestigious conference sites, nocturnal oases, contract offices, and French restaurants.
- CALL: "Feasible . . . within the limits of. . . ."

Forthright Fuzzifiers

- BEHAVIORAL PATTERNS: Specialize in fuzzifying where they stand on issues. Skillful constructors of semantical structures that are capable of multiple interpretation and appropriately full of rapidly adjustable holes. Forthright Fuzzifiers move with decisiveness and aggressiveness as they build their survival structures.
- PROFILES AND PLUMAGE: Conservative; brushed.
- HABITAT: Members of the species can be found in all types of bureaucracies around the world, but they are most common in governmental offices that deal with foreign or external affairs. Political speechwriters and drafters of Ph.D. dissertations are also among the most effective Fuzzifiers.
- CALL: "And, subject to a few minor qualifications, I believe. . . ."

- BEHAVIORAL PATTERNS: This species includes both domestic and international practitioners of the shredders' art. Telecomic Shredders are selective shredders of: (1) governmental documents for the adjustment of historical interpretation, and (2) shredders of other materials to insure domestic tranquility.
- PROFILES AND PLUMAGE: Intervenatory. Conservative plumage.
- HABITAT: Usually found roosting in the highest branches of governmental and corporate structures.
- CALL: Whisper-like "Shreddit, shreddit."

Telecomic Shredders

Fringeful Hoverers

Vago de los Ríos

- BEHAVIORAL PATTERNS: Bureaucrats with marginal thoughts and significant contacts, Fringeful Hoverers hover about the executive nests to sip of the rarified atmosphere and to eat the scraps from the head table. Status through proximity. Bag carriers and shoe shiners.
- PROFILES AND PLUMAGE: Eager profiles; frittering plumage of cavarian scavengers.
- HABITAT: Reception rooms of executives. Also often seen driving executives, running errands for the wives of executives, and greeter-tenders for social events hosted by executives. Some Fringeful Hoverers are excellent joke-laughers and airplane-meeters.
- CALL: The call varies with degrees of sophistication of the individual birds. Some sing: "Absolutely correct; a keen insight." Others, less sophisticated, sing the same tune with a slight change in lyrics: "You're right, Boss. You're so right."

 Ranting Ravens

- BEHAVIORAL PATTERNS: Middle-level bureaucrats who use aggressive paper shuffling and direct verbal communication patterns as background for getting what they want from colleagues and, occasionally, from superiors. They supplant logic with loud tonal patterns. Often successful in intimidating timid superiors in matters of personal importance to them. Promotion by rantation. Wings sometimes clipped.
- PROFILES AND PLUMAGE: Aggressive profile; wild plumage.
- HABITAT: Sighted in most bureaucracies.
- CALL: "I just want to remind you. . . ."

Chapter 9

GENUS
National Security Albatross

A genus of bureaucrats
who think they know
how to do
what they are told to do,
think they know why,
but do whatever it is they do,
because they were told to do it.

- BEHAVIORAL PROFILE: Nocturnal specialists in breaking and entering homes and offices to obtain personal and professional data to satisfy official or unofficial law breakers. Whereas common burglars carry small bags with burglar tools, Law and Order Burglars carry suitcases in which they carry burglar tools. Behavioral patterns are modified from time to time to accommodate instructions from above.
- PROFILES AND PLUMAGE: Low profile; plumage changed as necessary to facilitate each assigned burglary.
- HABITAT: Wherever assigned.
- CALL: "If we're caught. . . ."

☞ Law and Order Burglars

Vayo de los Ríos

☞ Covert Taxpayer-Watchers

- BEHAVIORAL PATTERNS: A species of bird that is nurtured by taxpayers for the purpose of watching taxpayers of their own and other nations. The ecology of bureaucracy is of great concern to the members of the intelligence community who depend upon the little bureaucratic birds to tell them what is not going on in the world. With this voidal information, the official intelligentsia use their analytical processes to determine what may have happened somewhere sometime, and thus retrogressively prove how correct they have been, and how happy the taxpayers should be to support their quiet war games, and taxpayers who may wear their hair long may be. . . . Covert Taxpayer-Watchers are fun to watch. They usually roost next to doors.
- PROFILES AND PLUMAGE: Attractively low profiles; plumage as required.
- HABITAT: Everywhere, but most commonly in quiet places equipped with headsets.
- CALL: "Got a match?"

Vago de los Rios

☛ Rubber-Gloved Nocturns

- BEHAVIORAL PATTERNS: Spooky tiptoers by night, but alternately mumble and sing by day. The members of this species are breaking and entering specialists who can also photograph private papers, plant electronic bugs, and perform other illegal acts as desired. Notoriously inept. When caught, left holding the bag.
- PROFILES AND PLUMAGE: Profile shadowy; plumage adjustive.
- HABITAT: Office and apartment buildings.
- CALL: "Shuuush."

Vayo de los Rios

Red-wigged Dialoguers

- BEHAVIORAL PATTERNS: Specialists in entering hospitals and other institutions to determine the potential singing range of former Lobbibirds who may become Songbirds. Nests are fabricated from shredded corporate documents.
- PROFILES AND PLUMAGE: Head plumage is modified with wiggistic materials to facilitate incognitian approaches. Profiles also adjustable.
- HABITAT: Hospitals by day; shredded nests by night.
- CALL: "Don't call. . . . don't call. . . ."

- BEHAVIORAL PATTERNS: The members of this species are highly placed arm twisters who extract illegal contributions from corporations and other sources using the quid pro quo quota system. They are able to convert dirty money for dirty purposes into clean money for the same purposes by the use of complicated money laundries. They tend to scatter money around nesting areas with abandon and are able to establish Stashed Cash Funds in other than the home nesting country. Possess poor memories.
- PROFILES AND PLUMAGE: High contact profiles; variable plumage.
- HABITAT: Hover around highly placed nests. Never found in pedestrian locations though they may participate in pedestrian activities in the upper branches of diseased trees.
- CALL: "And I'll see what I can do. . . ."

Freewheeling Extortionnaires

👆 Clipped-Wing Scapegoats

- BEHAVIORAL PATTERNS: Clipped-Wing Scapegoats are the final or near-final evolutionary stage of the National Security Albatross genus.
- PROFILES AND PLUMAGE: Profiles, sad; sometimes bitter. Plumage sometimes drops out when national security no longer serves as a security blanket.
- HABITAT: Some bailistically flutter while others unhappily mutter in ungilded cages. Final roosting place is usually high and dry.
- CALL: "Write me a letter; send it by mail. . . ."

- BEHAVIORAL PATTERNS: A wide-ranging species of agents that are available for rent on general assignments and can be wrapped in a compatible flag. Intelligence agency moonlighters, former agents, and thrill-seeking freelancers. Nest-egg requirements negotiable. Developing nations sometimes contract for Rent-an-Agents, but some heads of state hesitate to contract for services due to concern about domestic politics or personal survival.
- PROFILES AND PLUMAGE: Profiles often not as low as thought to be. Plumage adjustable and sometimes wiggistic.
- HABITAT: Everywhere.
- CALL: "At the cans at 2:00 a.m. . . . ."

 Star-Spangled Rent-an-Agent

Chapter 10

GENUS
Valiant Strivers

A genus of bureaucrats
who don't know what to do,
but hope they do the right thing
while trying to find out
what to do.

Jago de los Rios

Retiring Nightingales

- BEHAVIORAL PATTERNS: Females are the chief bureaucrats of home nests; males, aggressive away from the nest, are passive when in the nesting area. Female Retiring Nightingales are carefully preened and camouflaged when sighted during periods of public hovering, particularly if hovering at Wednesday Morning Study Club meetings, roosting with bridgebirds, or flocking at evening parties. It has been reported that a major transformation takes place when the females begin their nightly moulting, grease-packing, and headwrapping. Though most females wrap their heads in beauty-mummifying toilet tissue, some Retiring Nightingales prefer a type of floppy and grease-stained satin bag. The paper shortage in the world market appears to be stimulating increased baggification.
- PROFILES AND PLUMAGE: Variable by day, unknown by night. Only the mate of the Retiring Nightingale knows what the female really looks like.
- HABITAT: By day, everywhere. By early evening, elsewhere. By night, at home nest.
- CALL: "I'll be there in a minute. . . ."

Ecumemo Harmonizers

Vugo de los Ríos

- BEHAVIORAL PATTERNS: A species of clergybirds, sometimes known as cleribureaucrats, whose members believe that interfaith harmony is vital to the defense of cleribureaucracy. Ecumemo Harmonizers are devoted exchangers of memoranda, and they have been known to conduct international memofests. Each memorandum avoids controversy and is carefully written in terms that reflect orthodoxy in issue minimality. Ecumemo Harmonizers love to congregate.
- PROFILES AND PLUMAGE: Large profiles; conservative plumage. Coloration: black, brown, grey, and highly neutral.
- HABITAT: Religious institutions of all types. Also commonly sighted in airports and on airplanes; the species can always be found in conferences where they exchange memoranda and participate in lengthy dialogues in which they define and redefine terms.
- CALL: "Perhaps another conference. . . ."

- BEHAVIORAL PATTERNS: A senior and sophisticated cousin of the American Postabird, a country bird. Canadian Postacoders design, code, and scramble the postal codes of Canada. Between eras of coding, the members of the species try to teach the taxpayers how to develop jingles to help them remember their "Letter-Number-Letter (Space) Number-Letter-Number" postal (zip) codes.* Canadian Postacoders smile when they do it, while the U.S. coders frown. Though the Canadian mail is delivered more rapidly than the U.S. mail, the Canadian Postacoders ultimately may develop their art sufficiently to catch up with the slowness of the U.S. mail.
- PROFILES AND PLUMAGE: Unknown. No one has ever admitted being a postacoder.
- HABITAT: In a highly classified site in, near, or around Ottawa.
- CALL: To the tune of "Jingle Bells": "Juggle mail, juggle mail, juggle all the way. Oh, what fun the folks will have, when the mail gets through some day."

*See *American Postabirds, Genus Boxed Pigeons.*

Canadian
Postacoders

Vago de los Ríos

Vago de los Ríos

👉 Physical Culture Birds

- BEHAVIORAL PATTERNS: Young birds strive to develop their physical assets for public preening while older birds take specialized exercises in vain attempts to regain their lost youth. Reformed female libbers can be sighted quietly straining to reaffirm the formerly unsupportive pectoral muscularities. Males often begin muscular development programs to impress females, however, they often revert to mirroristic interest in self-imaging.
- PROFILES AND PLUMAGE: Females show well-developed rumperatory regions and males show full muscle development from the ankles to between the ears. Plumage of females is randomly prolific while the plumage of males tends to be sparse. Balding males often comb the growth of the left sideburns over the head and to the right side.
- HABITAT: YMCA, YWCA, exercise salons, and self-defense classes.
- CALL: Almost inaudible grunts.

👉 Calling Card Starlings

- BEHAVIORAL PATTERNS: Constantly traveling in an effort to sell themselves and their commodities, Calling Card Starlings leave their calling cards wherever they flutter.
- PROFILES AND PLUMAGE: Vigorous profile; rakish plumage.
- HABITAT: Status, plus eagerness to conquer new territories, cause the members of the species to flit from office to office and hallway to hallway. Primarily found in corporate bureaucracies, they are prolific card droppers.
- CALL: "Just an initial order . . . ; About eight thirty tonight. . . ."

Chapter 11

GENUS
Mumbling Songbirds

A genus of bureaucrats
who know what to do,
know how to do it,
don't care,
and would rather sing about it
than do it.

— Vago de los Ríos

👉 Marathon Mumblebirds

- BEHAVIORAL PATTERNS: Quick to learn new buzz words of new executives above them, but unable to tie the buzz words to meaningful propositions. Listeners tend to interpret the mumbling to mean whatever they wish it to mean; this adjustive interpretation contributes to the popularity of the species.
- PROFILES AND PLUMAGE: No established profile since Marathon Mumblebirds can be found in all shapes and sizes. Plumage variable.
- HABITAT: Found everywhere, but most commonly in receiving lines or at dining tables where they mumble introductions.
- CALL: Low-volume mumbling with a mixture of both linear and vertical mumbling.

🖐 Celebating Hoot Owls

- BEHAVIORAL PATTERNS: Noisy but unproductive bureaucrats whose principal characteristics are unsteady roosting, loud and boastful hoots, and no performance. Usually found at middle levels of governmental bureaucracies. Lay many eggs, all infertile.
- PROFILES AND PLUMAGE: Large head, large body, large eyes, broad posterior; heavy plumage with conservative coloration.
- HABITAT: Primarily a governmental nester, the Celebating Hoot Owl can be found at national and local level institutions, but extend their roosting periods to include sippistic intakes at near-office oases.
- CALL: The call of the Celebating Hoot Owls opens with three hoots, followed by a mushily articulated song to the tune of "Show me the way to go home." "Hand me the regulations; I know all the ways to say no. I killed a policy about an hour ago, and I saved the status quo."

Vuyo de los Rios

👉 Nocturnal Teasers

- BEHAVIORAL PATTERNS: Males can be recognized by their constantly roving eyes and occasional tendency to pinch nearby females. Females can be identified by their constant preening and regular dousing of their bodies with commercial perfumes. As dinner hour approaches, the behavior patterns of the female include eye rolling, eyelash (real or modified) fluttering, tail twitching, and romantic cooing. Following dinner and wine, the behavior reverts to frosty inaction. Nonperformers.
- PROFILES AND PLUMAGE: Well-arranged.
- HABITAT: Found everywhere.
- CALL: By day, the members of this species mumble with cautious non-directiveness. By night, the males mumble softly and with tonal notes that range with a questioning slur from middle "C" to upper "E-flat." Females are noted for pre-meal coos that become post-meal noos.

👉 Dangling Showbirds

- BEHAVIORAL PATTERNS: Dangling Showbirds are performing artists who sign contracts with producers but who must dangle through three days of rehearsals before the previously signed contracts become valid. Most of the species are happy cooperators who are transformed into Insatiable Egobirds as soon as they survive the three-day period of dangling (known as the *dangling jangledays*). Producers often exhibit the same behavioral characteristics as Dangling Showbirds.
- PROFILES AND PLUMAGE: No pattern.
- HABITAT: Found in the behind-the-curtains bureaucracy of show business which binds lights, stage mikes, makeup, and effervescent egos in high-tension red tape, wraps it all in contractual paper, and files it in combustion-oriented green rooms.
- CALL: During the dangling jangledays, the Showbirds coo with cooperative softness. Those who fail to survive the dangling jangledays usually explode with shriekistic singing about the judgment of producers who do not recognize the showbirds' artistry. Producers sometimes shriek, but more often they sing mumblingly low while exhibiting the behavior patterns of Stomper-Outers who leave rehearsals with the commercial harmonics of resounding stompisms.

85

🖐 Insatiable Egobirds

- **BEHAVIORAL PATTERNS:** Insatiable Egobirds have a mirror outlook on their role in society and the obligations of society as related to their role. The orbital causations are centered in the insufficiently heralded importance of the species. Authors and comedians take on the coloration of Insatiable Egobirds when appearing on radio and television talk shows. This results in interesting interfacing of halos as the host-guest dialogues provide the tonal background for the competitive placement of ego-halos.
- **PROFILES AND PLUMAGE:** Usually in a fully puffed state. Tail feathers preened and sprayed with fixative. Plumage usually is the finest product of the dyers' art.
- **HABITAT:** Most Insatiable Egobirds are performers on various stages: they can be found flitting around all types of bureaucracies. They may be politicians, political appointees, diplomats, artists, management consultants, professors, critics, insurance company adjusters, and statuesque bodies.
- **CALL:** The call of the Insatiable Egobirds always rhymes with the letters of their initials . . . i.e., I.E. The calls usually begin with: "I personally believe . . . ; I had a funny thing happen to me . . . ; I don't know why I felt the way I did, but I did . . . ; As for me . . . ; If it hadn't been for me. . . ."

(Genny Boles, actress and ornibureaucratologist, has described an age-old test for Insatiable Ego birds in show business: "Enough about me. What did *you* think of my last performance?")

Chapter 12

GENUS
Calculating Boodlebirds

A genus of bureaucrats
who know what to do,
know how to do it,
and do it to others.

Haquing Hatchetbirds

- BEHAVIORAL PATTERNS: A haquistic political bureaucrat (polibu) who serves as the between-elections keeper of the records. With black book in hand, the HH records favors delivered and tribute received, thus maintaining constant surveillance over the debit-credit facts of public life. In post-election days, the Haquing Hatchetbirds recodify personnel policies and supervise personnel assignments. They orchestrate assignments based on a careful analysis of appointees' political pedigrees, political endorsements and devotion to the principles of in-house boodling. Some hatchetbirds, like butcherbirds, cast their castees (rejects) into thorny problem areas, and they sometimes leave them to swing slowly in the breezes of frustration.
- PROFILES AND PLUMAGE: Low
- HABITAT: Often found in small offices adjoining the offices of cabinet officials, governors, mayors, and chairmen of political parties. Also can be sighted in hotel suites of lobbibirds.
- CALL: "Who sent you???? Don't call me, I'll call you . . . ; Leave your resume . . . ; We have a new assignment for you . . . ; The Boss will issue a statement that he accepts your resignation with regret. . . ."

- BEHAVIORAL PATTERNS: Fossils of Acupuncturing Buddibirds have been found with those of cockroaches and other related forms of life, thus indicating that the species is probably one of the earliest members of *Familia Bureaucratica*. Acupuncturing Buddibirds promote their own careers with skillful surgical instrumentation. Some, however, do not use the knife, but depend on very timely implants of specialized praise and carefully poised omissions. Some AB's slash their way to the top while others fall flat on their own instrumentation.
- PROFILES AND PLUMAGE: Smiling profile . . . with balancing retention of one hand behind the back. Plumage variable.
- HABITAT: Though found in academic faculties and in communications media, Acupuncturing Buddibirds are particularly numerous in corporate, governmental, and religious bureaucracies. Though commonly thought to be most effective in corporate and governmental bureaucracies, the Acupuncturing Buddibirds are most abundant and skillful in the institutions of religious bureaucracies. Assignments, commission placements, and travel opportunities provide avenues for articulate buddibirding.
- CALL: "I've never heard him say anything bad about you . . . ; After all, he's had a lot of problems lately . . . ; She's usually pretty good about . . . ; I prayed about it. . . ."

☞ Acupuncturing Buddibirds

Vago de los Ríos

Vago de los Ríos

👉 Mumbling Polibus

- BEHAVIORAL PATTERNS: Normally roosting in political arenas where local, regional, and national politicians are traditionally found, Mumbling Polibus are usually elected office-holders but many are staff members. Can be identified by the forthright indecisiveness of position as indicated in letters, press releases, and public statement. Are particularly compatible with Genus Bugling Flaques. Always speaking, but never listen to each other.
- PROFILES AND PLUMAGE: Posed. Guarded.
- HABITAT: Usually found on fences, or as guests of yachtsmen or Lobbibirds.
- CALL: "Thank you for your views . . . ; In regard to your problem, I am pleased to enclose a letter from the Department of . . . ; I need to get away for a few days. . . ."

- BEHAVIORAL PATTERNS: Feeding primarily on latex-ualized chicken or cold barbecue served in flexible paper plates that permit the species to play games with rolling peas, the American Polibu has proliferated through the years. Some have gained in-house reputations as outstanding pea-controllers, but some of the species have a tendency to permit pea-droppings while shaking hands with potential supporters. Characterized by eyes that are alert to voter recognition and hands that tingle with anticipatory sensitiveness at the sight of a campaign contributor. In restaurants, constantly table-hop and hand-pump.
- PROFILES AND PLUMAGE: Normally a paunchistic profile. Most American Polibus fondle cigars. When angry, the pasty complexion appears to take on a healthy ruddiness. Plumage either sparse or glued.
- HABITAT: Range throughout the United States; can be found wherever there is a free trip or wherever twenty or more voters may be gathered. At gatherings of voters, the American Polibus gush with mumblistic recall of names.
- CALL: "I promise you . . . ; As soon as we know the final form of the bill . . . ; Fiscal responsibility, fiscal responsibility."

☞ American Polibu

👉 Star Spangled Polibu

Vago de los Ríos

- BEHAVIORAL PATTERNS: The distinction between the Star Spangled Polibu and the American Polibu is difficult for new bureaucrat-watchers to make. Feeding and liquificating habits appear to be identical, but the Star Spangled Polibus jump a little higher when the national flag appears, sing a little louder (with facial gesturing) when the national anthem is sung, and wrap the flag about their motives with greater flourishes when members of veterans organizations are in the nesting, feeding, or liquificating area. Canadian Polibus sometimes appear to have the same characteristics as Star Spangled Polibus, but the maplistic wrapping material sometimes shows slight union jackistic traces when the Canadian Polibu is in the presence of super-royalized voters.
- PROFILES AND PLUMAGE: Same as the American Polibu. Paunchistic. Plumage sparse or glued.
- HABITAT: At all gatherings of voters but particularly at gatherings of older veterans.
- CALL: "We must bring back. . . ."

- BEHAVIORAL PATTERNS: Maximize national identity, particularly in the fields of literature and the performing arts. Many Canadian Polibus are positive buglers who call lagging attention to the work of Canadian writers, painters, and performers. Canadian Polibus are bilingual mumblers while their U.S. cousins sometimes only approach monolingual capability. Whereas the American Polibus wrap themselves in their flag, the Canadian Polibus are often cautious flag-wrappers, because the war-of-the-flags has left pockets of voter sensitization.
- PROFILES AND PLUMAGE: Lively.
- HABITAT: Found wherever there are gatherings of people or cameras/microphones.
- CALL: "In these trying times. . . ."

 Canadian
Polibus

☞ Dull-Eyed
Tickerbirds

Vago de los Ríos

- BEHAVIORAL PATTERNS: Eyes are usually scanning ticker-tapes, wall charts, financial pages of papers, annual reports, and activities of certain fellow-tickerbirds. Make extensive use of the telephone, dine well, and sit all day in a variety of chairs. It has been reported that in 1949, a Dull-Eyed Tickerbird read a book.
- PROFILES AND PLUMAGE: Settled profile. Plumage sparse or pasted.
- HABITAT: Can be sighted silently flocking in medium to large rooms that are equipped with chairs, an electronic wall chart, and cigar smoke. Occasionally can be seen fluttering to banks.
- CALL: "Harrrumph. Buy . . . ; Harrrumph. Sell. . . ."

- BEHAVIORAL PATTERNS: Sightings of males are quite common but female Potbellied Pinchers are rarely seen, because they tend to practice their pinching in the nest. Males are promiscuous pinchers; pinching is randomly directed; selection of target is by opportunity. Potbellied Pinchers focus their activities on the laggistic or rumperatorical portions of the female birds of various species. Potbellied Pinchers are equal opportunity pinchers.
- PROFILES AND PLUMAGE: Females are of various sizes and shapes. Males tend to be older birds who have a maximized paunch. Plumage: none to sparse. For females, the plumage is in question; usually wrapped in toilet tissue or satin baggies.
  - HABITAT: Males are most readily seen pinching in offices, elevators, and oases in the nesting area. Females pinch privately in the nest.
  - CALL: "Nice...."

Potbellied
Pinchers

Vago de los Ríos

Vago de los Ríos

Rumperatory Tinglecoots

- BEHAVIORAL PATTERNS: A species of bureaucrat whose male members have a visual fixation on the laggistic anatomical structure of female tinglecoots and other birds. Males of the species often experience a tingling sensation in the hand and fingers when in the visual range of females. Females are programmed to gaze coyly over their shoulders occasionally at male observers and walk with a hitheristic orbitting of the rumperatory structure.
- PROFILES AND PLUMAGE: Variable.
- HABITAT: Fledgling Rumperatory Tinglecoots can be found in schools, swimming pools, and churches. Mature members of the species can be found wherever bureaucrats feed, nest, or play.
- CALL: Fledgling Rumperatory Tinglecoots sing after-thoughts in semantical echo patterns that reflect current programming, but old Tinglecoots sing marginal after-thoughts that are more memorial in nature than current. "Oooooooo."

Rumperatory Coots

Vago de los Ríos

- BEHAVIORAL PATTERNS: Closely related to Rumperatory Tinglecoots. Male members of this species are cautiously aggressive, and females are primly passive. Other patterns of behavior are identical to those of Rumperatory Tinglecoots.*
- PROFILES AND PLUMAGE: Males of Rumperatory Coots have few tail feathers, while the males of Tinglecoots have broad fantails that twitch in excitation, and fingers that tingle in anticipation. Females have slightly rumpled tail feathers. Multicolored plumage.
- HABITAT: Found in most offices, department stores, and elevators. In summer months, flock at beaches.
- CALL: "Oooooo." (Lower octave than the "Oooooo" of the Rumperatory Tinglecoots.)

  *There is disagreement among leading ornibureaucratologists about the classification of Coots and Tinglecoots. Some authorities blieve the two are totally different species while others believe that Coots are actually Tinglecoots who have lost their fantails from extended periods of twitching. Dr. Glenn P. Wilson, who has made a major study of tail-twitching, believes "once a coot, always a coot." In his unpublished study, Wilson makes a scholarly argument for classifying both Tinglecoots and Coots simply as Coots. Coots, he believes, are Tinglecoots who have been ravaged by time and experiential excess. The Boren position is one of forthright neutrality.

- BEHAVIORAL PATTERNS: Females are dominant in the species, and tend to rule the roost where found. In most offices, females of the species really perform whatever duties are performed though the Bossbird receives the pay, title, and other emoluments of the position. Females can be observed constantly turning their heads to survey every action in the office, and they often flit from desk to desk to inspect the work of Timidbirds. Known to shriek demands at their bosses who can't fire them, female Rulingbirds are the only ones who know what the Bossbirds are supposed to do and how to do it. Brassy Rulingbirds and Titular Bossbirds have a dominating-accommodating understanding. Females are also dominant in the home, but they normally permit the male to appear to be dominant.
- PROFILES AND PLUMAGE: Variable.
- HABITAT: Found in all types of offices in all types of bureaucracies around the world.
- CALL: "Now, listen to me. . . ."

☞ Brassy Rulingbirds

Vago de los Ríos

 Senior Lobbibirds

- BEHAVIORAL PATTERNS: Senior Lobbibirds establish a level of understanding that permits appropriate consideration of their clients' problems in a quid proistic basis. When huddling or coveying with officials, the Senior Lobbibirds can be observed holding a glass in one hand and alternately putting their other hand in their own and other people's pockets. Many of the species thrushily retire to plush nests where they dance the dissipated shuffle to a syncopated beat. Noted for large expense accounts.
- PROFILES AND PLUMAGE: Heavily settled profile. Sparsifying plumage.
- HABITAT: Found roosting around legislative and administrative offices of all levels of government. Also frequent oases and expensive restaurants.
- CALL: "By the way, . . . ; Just a little matter that. . . ."

Chapter 13

GENUS
Authoritative Gigglebirds

A genus of bureaucrats
who don't know what to do,
but sing and hover
as if they do.

- BEHAVIORAL PATTERNS: A type of mammal that is related to vampire bats, the License Tag Dingbats thrive on the body fluids that are spilled by taxpayers who stand in long lines and who mumble as they slowly shuffle to the counter where the extractions are made. Contrary to popular conception, there are as many male Dingbats as there are female Dingbats.
- PROFILES AND PLUMAGE: Hungry. Silky.
- HABITAT: Usually found as employees in state, provincial, and county offices that dispense license tags for various types of vehicles. The members of the species stay in the dark most of the time, and are noted for their upside-down thinking.
- CALL: Inaudible.

 License Tag Dingbats

Vago de los Ríos

Vago de los Rios

👉 Sonorous Posicators

- BEHAVIORAL PATTERNS: Sonorous Posicators (pose-i-cators) are public or private sector bureaucrats who are professional posers of questions. Posicators are proficient in using dependent clauses as a means of extending non-question questions into marathon exercises that cause the person to be questioned mumblingly to agree ("in general terms") rather than ask that the question be asked again or clarified. Both males and females are among the most noted Posicators.
- PROFILES AND PLUMAGE: Profiles, disturbing. Plumage, forgettable.
- HABITAT: To be found in all bureaucracies; most often sighted in community meetings, professional or trade association conferences, and faculty meetings.
- CALL: "Do I understand you to be saying. . . ."

103

Titular Bossbirds

- BEHAVIORAL PATTERNS: Titular Bossbirds possess the title and receive all the emoluments of being a boss, but they are the boss in name only. Some Titular Bossbirds know of their titular status, accept it, and play the game of diffused management. They normally find an effective Brassy Rulingbird to do whatever it is that the Bossbird is supposed to do if it can be determined. Some Titular Bossbirds, however, really think they are running things but everyone else in the office, on the board, and the organization's clients know that he is not the true boss. TBs participate in board meetings, preside over meetings that are run by others, and play golf or attend business conventions. (If the Titular Bossbird is a male, and if he is married, the wife is placed in a difficult status situation. Most wives of Titular Bossbirds know the husband is titularized but do not want to let the husband know they know.)
- PROFILES AND PLUMAGE: Profile, pompous. Plumage, well trimmed.
- HABITAT: Found in corporate bureaucracies and, to a lesser extent, can be sighted in governmental offices.
- CALL: "Just give it to Ms. . . . ; Now, the new policy of the office will be. . . ."

104

- BEHAVIORAL PATTERNS: When flocking with other birds, Nosistic Snobbingbirds practice nose-aiming and diaphragmic utterances. Mature birds can't do anything, but can serve as advisors to those who can. All Nosistic Snobbingbirds are proficient yes-butters who amble with majestic uniformity and thoughtful minimality.
- PROFILES AND PLUMAGE: Profiles of maximized formality and nose-aiming. Plumage adjustive.
- HABITAT: Often found listed on payrolls as professors, diplomats, investment bankers, and management consultants. Fledglings are most frequently sighted as apprentice diplomats.
- CALL: Diaphragmic utterance: "Perhaps."

Nosistic Snobbingbirds

Vago de los Ríos

Opulescent Joggingbirds

- BEHAVIORAL PATTERNS: A wide-ranging species whose broad interests are derived from nagging spouses and a love for caloric optimization. The illogical interfaces result in corpulent excess, or simply too much fat. Military officers and corporate contractors occasionally jog together by day and share their thoughts by night while recovering from the jogging by eating and drinking. Old joggers never die; they just jiggle away.
- PROFILES AND PLUMAGE: Profiles maximized with saggistic tendencies. Plumage tousled.
- HABITAT: Found in all bureaucracies.
- CALL: "Huhhh, uhhhh, huhhh, uhhhh, huhhh."

 Neighborhood
Poseyrangers

- BEHAVIORAL PATTERNS: Females of all ages can be seen fluttering between flower beds and weed lots to gather and prepare materials for the nest. Males tend the flower beds upon retirement. Species is characterized by institutionalized flocking at which time the birds cluck and sing as they view dead vegetation sticking out of bottles. Behind the unruffled plumage of tranquil amity beat hearts of fierce competition.
- PROFILES AND PLUMAGE: Eager profile; carefully arranged plumage.
- HABITAT: Found in every neighborhood. Flock together on local, national, and international basis.
- CALL: "Ahhhhh, oooooo, mmmmmm."

Vago de los Ríos

Vago de los Ríos

👉 Crusty-Feathered Profundicator

(Also known as the Ivy League Profundifier.)

- BEHAVIORAL PATTERNS: By means of thesauric enrichment, constructive emulation, and multisyllabitic buzzwords, the members of this species can translate simple ideas into complex patterns of conceptual rhetoric. Though no new substance is added to profundicated messages, the Crusty-Feathered Profundicators can make a stirring contribution to the bureaucratic environment. Profundicators normally pump their heads as they project their pellets of ineffable thoughts into organized collections. Some Profundicators become submerged in their own profundication.
- PROFILES AND PLUMAGE: Diggistic profiles; crusty plumage.
- HABITAT: Can be found in all types of bureaucracies.
- CALL: "Whewwwww."

- BEHAVIORAL PATTERNS: Fuzzy-Headed Tapebirds are management analysts who happily weave procedural red tape as they move from office to office to analyze whatever it is that the office does. Some members of the species not only weave available scraps of red tape into bandages that bind hypothetical hernias or other organizational weak spots but they also are able to produce original tape of their own. Some are not weavers but quilters who use available scraps to develop heavy blanketing quilts. Fuzzy-Headed Tapebirds usually carry clipboards under one arm to try to project a pattern of total authority and organizational concern.
- PROFILES AND PLUMAGE: Downy headfeathers, thrusting beaks, and waddling profile.
- HABITAT: Fuzzy-Headed Tapebirds are in-house birds in most governmental, corporate, and academic bureaucracies, but are often found as management echosultants in smaller organizations that wish to find reasons for firing some people and hiring friends or relatives.
- CALL: "How do *you* think things are going?"

☞ Fuzzy-Headed Tapebirds

Vago de los Rios

Bureaucratic Tapecutters

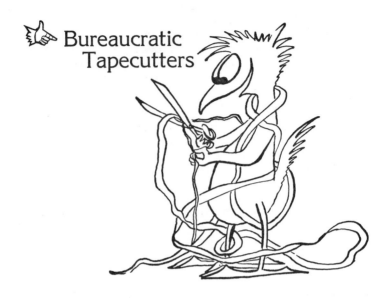

- BEHAVORIAL PATTERNS: Related to Fuzzy-Headed Tapebirds, the Bureaucratic Tapecutters are specialists in cutting red tape, but in keeping with proper bureaucratic traditions, the red tape is cut lengthwise. Tapebirds from the United States, Canada, Mexico, France, Brazil, Jamaica, and Peru are seeking United Nations approval for an international conference on cutting red tape. (They are convinced that if lengthwise cutting of red tape can be expedited, enough red tape could be produced to envelop the earth in a protective cushion that would assure the earth's survival in any future inter-planetary collision. The UN resolution would encourage all nations to place lengthwise tapecutting as the number one priority for the use of all economic resources*.)
- PROFILES AND PLUMAGE: Profile, settled. Plumage, fuzzy.
- HABITAT: Bureaucratic Tapebirds are found in all bureaucracies.
- CALL: "Lengthwise, yes; crosswise, no."

*The tapebird flying from London to Paris for the planning sessions became entangled in its own red tape and did not survive the flight over the English Channel.

 Urbanito's Chichabirds

- BEHAVIORAL PATTERNS: First classified by the late Urban P. Wittig, a noted bird-watcher and ornibureaucratologist. Chichabirds tolerate and look with quiet sympathy upon low-flying but high-buzzing representatives or foundations and development organizations that specialize in community development hovering. Chichabirds seek to guard chichabird culture and chichabird values from the disruptive intrusions of foreign developers. The foreign developers seek to homogenize the behavioral patterns of chichabirds, but development malfunctions sometimes result in skimming the cultural cream and leave chichabirds with skim culture. After extended periods of contact, many chichabirds give up.
- PROFILES AND PLUMAGE: Profiles range from variable verticality to steadfast stancing. Plumage sometimes plastered, sometimes frazzled with abandonment.
- HABITAT: Normally found in Andean villages and concentrated around small adobe buildings that signal the availability of in-season chicha, a demasticated corn brew for domesticated birds. Closely related to the Andean Chichabirds are the cachaçabirds of rural Brazil.
- CALL: "Salud!"

Chapter 14

GENUS
Dedicated Botchers

A genus of bureaucrats
who don't know what to do,
think they do,
but do the wrong thing.

Vago de los Rios

Retrogressive Dodoputers
(dō-dō-pu-ters)

- BEHAVIORAL PATTERNS: The brains of the Retrogressive Dodoputers function as a digital computer; all factors are based on historical or pasttified* data. Dodoputers tend to think, live, and predict with clarity of rear view vision, and they move with unclutchable and unbrakeable reverse speed. Characterized by tailistic leadership and nosistic steerage.
- PROFILES AND PLUMAGE: Profiles, backwards; plumage, wild.
- HABITAT: Found in all bureaucracies and most often nest in fiscal offices.
- CALL: "To the rear, . . ."

---

*Professional bureaucrats rely heavily on pasttified data—data that is randomly collected from old sources. The older, the better. Analytical processes based on pasttification give warmth and comfort to bureaucrats who prefer tranquility by old data to accuracy by current data.

- BEHAVIORAL PATTERNS: With little, if any, experiential background to disturb their analytical processes, Puffed Fledglings take concerted action toward partially defined objectives. Some of the species remain fledgings all their lives and show little evidence of evolutionary or educative improvement.
- PROFILES AND PLUMAGE: Enervated profiles; way-out plumage.
- HABITAT: Found in all bureaucracies in nearly all nations of the world, but appear to be most heavily concentrated in the academic bureaucracies. Many of the species are not officially attached to any bureaucratic institutions, but are believed by some ornibureaucratologists to be in need of some institutional relationships. Free-floating birds.
- CALL: "Under thirty, good. Over thirty, bad."

🖝 Puffed Fledglings

Vago de los Ríos

Vago de los Ríos

👉 Pyramiding Featherheads

- BEHAVIORAL PATTERNS: Members of this species devote most of their efforts to enlarging their nests and proliferating their species. They make regular migrations to management conferences where they exchange organizational charts and autograph procedural manuals. Always busy.
- PROFILES AND PLUMAGE: Eager profiles; fringeful plumage.
- HABITAT: Most readily found in the highest branches of the management structure of all institutions; sightings may be made at middle management levels as well. A universal bureaucrat, because found in all bureaucracies.
- CALL: "By expanding the division. . . ."

116

Jago de los Ríos

No-Sign Roadplanners

- BEHAVIORAL PATTERNS: Specialists in designing roads that confuse motorists due to the lack of signs, the No-Sign Roadplanners devote their energies and the taxpayers' money to building roads that will let the travelers enjoy no-sign scenery as they rush to wherever they may not be going. The species is made up of happy birds.
- PROFILES AND PLUMAGE: Profiles, happy; Plumage, abandoned.
- HABITAT: No-Sign Roadplanners are to be found primarily in capital cities.
- CALL: "Loopytiloop, loopytiloop."

117

Vago de los Ríos

👉 Personnelbirds

- BEHAVIORAL PATTERNS: The Personnelbirds sing great arias about the ladderistically ineffable programs for classifying, assigning, and promoting. Distinguished paper shufflers. Devoted guardians of equitable procedures, this species is able to adjustify procedures when they are ordered to do so by associated Lobbibirds or The Boss. Some Personnelbirds have studied data processing techniques and have learned to compute decision postponement.
- PROFILES AND PLUMAGE: Ordinary.
- HABITAT: Though some religious and academic bureaucracies profess to have professional Personnelbirds in their organizations, most genuine Personnelbirds are to be found in governmental and corporate institutions.
- CALL: "Wheeeeeeeee."

Blue-footed Libbers

- BEHAVIORAL PATTERNS: A newly developing species in which the males are dominated by female chauvinists. Females show aggressive interest in career-oriented parity; males seek equal rights at home.
- PROFILE AND PLUMAGE: Females range from high-breasted to unsupportive expansionisms while males tend to have a settling profile. Plumage is variable but less wiggistic than with most birds.
- HABITAT: Found in corporate, governmental, and academic nesting areas. Very few sighted in cleribureaucracies. Females rarely at home due to tendency to flock together for mutually reinforcing clucking.
- CALL: A wide variety of tones characterize the singing of this species. Males make sounds by timid chest thumping, but females all shriekily sing the same song: "Male chauvinist pigs, male chauvinist pigs." During singing periods, the toes of females appear to be clutchistic and somewhat rigid.

Chapter 15

GENUS
Broadtailed Fingertappers

A genus of bureaucrats
who know what to do,
know how to do it,
are given a chance to do it,
but don't do anything.

☞ Knitpicking Vultures*

- BEHAVIORAL PATTERNS: Scavengers of whatever is left after well-connected bureaucrats have picked over the variously more pleasing assignments. Effective instruments of the status quo and bare-bones analysis. Never innovate but consistently interpolate.
- PROFILES AND PLUMAGE: Have an ecological or no-litter view of the world that is reflected in their scanning and lobing searches. Haunchy stance for searching. Plumage somewhat olfactorical; essences of a *carnivore* nature.
- HABITAT: All bureaucracies.
- CALL: "Uuuulp, uuuulp."

* Not to be confused with nitpickers that deal primarily with the eggs of lice. Knitpicking involves a more stylized and professional type of bone picking.

Pondering Eagles

- BEHAVIORAL PATTERNS: Quick to assert legal dominion but slow to make substantive pronouncements. Nests are cluttered with open books, yellow pads, ulcer medications, and empty bottles. Secretaries to Pondering Eagles perform much of the professional work with minimal recognition and pay.
- PROFILES AND PLUMAGE: Oratorical but settled profile. Plumage expensive.
- HABITAT: In all bureaucracies but tend to specialize their pondering in and around the Office of the General Counsel.
- CALL: If hurried, Pondering Eagles sing "No." If given unlimited time, they may ultimately sing "Maybe." No member of the species has ever yet been heard to sing an unequivocal "Yes."

Vago de los Rios

☞ Exalted Chairpersons

- BEHAVIORAL PATTERNS: Exalted Chairpersons usually submerge their limited abilities in the wide-ranging and in-depth attention to rules of procedure. Males fumble with pipes and pipe cleaners, and females are normally seen making periodic dives into bulging purses. Mumbling sessions are periods of modified meanderings through which some conferees are able to hang dozily on to marginal consciousness until the sessions are ended in closing grunts by the Chairperson. Conference Doodlers thrive well under the orchestrated inactivity of Exalted Chairpersons.
- PROFILES AND PLUMAGE: Conservative baggy-elbowed garments that blend well with droopy profiles.
- HABITAT: Sighted in all bureaucracies from the home to the presidential palaces, Exalted Chairpersons orchestrate at the end of tables equipped with yellow pads and doodling pencils.
- CALL: "Any other comments?"

- BEHAVIORAL PATTERNS: Very active and tend to be nondirective in emphasis. Bumbling Bullfinches strut pompously about their nests and scatter paper and other materials of the profession around the nesting areas. An eager strutter that messes up its own nest while pondering The Big Picture.
- PROFILES AND PLUMAGE: Pompous.
- HABITAT: Found in all bureaucracies but most common in academic and religious institutions.
- CALL: "In a broad sense. . . ."

☞ Bumbling Bullfinches

Chapter 16

GENUS
Happy Shufflebirds

A genus of bureaucrats
who know what to do,
know how to do it,
but interpret whatever they want to do
to be what they should do,
and do it.

👉 Academic Paperthrashers

- BEHAVIORAL PATTERNS: Academic bureaucrats who love to scratch in paper of all sizes and shapes. Both male and female Academic Paperthrashers sing of their dislike for paper while secretly thrilling to the shufflistic sounds. Paper grading, paper reading, paper drafting, paper routing, and the orchestration of administrative memoranda, PTA bulletins, questionnaires, and grade reports are but part of the inspiring shufflisms that help convince teachers that they are professionals.
- PROFILES AND PLUMAGE: Very conservative except at distant educational conferences.
- HABITAT: Heavy nesting in all classrooms but particularly to be found in offices of registrars, deans, development officers, and business managers.
- CALL: "Wish I had time to teach . . . ; Wish I had time to administer. . . ." (Very low volume but gleeful noises may be heard during student registration periods.)

- BEHAVIORAL PATTERNS: An evening species. Males are minimally melonized and rarely seen. Females possess a profile of willingness and cooperation and are seen a great deal. Females tend to moult easily after office hours.
- PROFILES AND PLUMAGE: Profile of willingness; plumage sparse at all times.
- HABITAT: Found in corporate, academic, and governmental nests. Also frequently sighted at business conferences of professional and trade associations.
- CALL: "OOOooaaooOOO, OOOooaaooOO."

☞ Melonbreasted Moulters

Vago de los Ríos

- BEHAVIORAL PATTERNS: The guardians of the status quo. Policy Homogenizers are found in middle-level groups that quickly adopt new policies from above, adjust the new policies through the use of new terms, and gradually adjustify and homogenize the new policies to be in harmony with the old policies. Policy Homogenizers assure that all new policies emerge from the bureaucratic tract homogenized so as to reflect little or no alteration from the old policy.
- PROFILES AND PLUMAGE: Conservative.
- HABITAT: All bureaucracies support Policy Homogenizers even though they may not have the title of Homogenizers.
- CALL: No normal bird call, only intestinal gurgling.

☞ Policy Homogenizers

👉 Ledger Buzzards

- BEHAVIORAL PATTERNS: The guardians of the accounts and delayers of purchase orders, Ledger Buzzards are conservative in demeanor until they gather in conventions with other buzzards at which time they share output with expansiveness. Ledger Buzzards are surpassed only by Pondering Eagles in the variety of ways that they can say no to colleagues in any bureaucracy.
- PROFILES AND PLUMAGE: A *don't-bother-me, I'm-busy* profile. Plumage variable but often covered in the forelock area by a green eyeshade.
- HABITAT: Found in all bureaucracies.
- CALL: "Put it in the box . . ."; "Can't do it now; later. . . ."

131

Vago de los Ríos

👉 Scrawlinitial Grouse

- BEHAVIORAL PATTERNS: Most activities of the Scrawl-initial Grouse are directed toward protecting their established territory. Though the mature bird does not know what to do or how to do it, it will not permit other birds to do it in their territory. They insist on scrawling their initials on all documents, buck slips, purchase orders, outgoing messages, and other paper in order to protect their domain to do whatever it is that they are supposed to do whenever they find out what it is and if they feel like doing it.
- PROFILES AND PLUMAGE: Busy profile; cautious plumage.
- HABITAT: Scrawlinitialing can be found in all bureaucracies, but predominates in governmental and corporate bureaucracies.
- CALL: Grousing, the official singing of the species, can be heard in all bureaucracies. Some beginning bureaucrats who do not have the authority to initial papers become soprano or tenor grousers long before they have the authority to initial.

- BEHAVIORAL PATTERNS: Bubbling Talkingbirds are the rapid transit system for news and rumors within any bureaucratic organization. Information is usually transmitted on a one-to-one basis in whispered monotones interrupted by gigglistic outbursts. Canadian Curlers bubble loudly as Sweepers sweep. All Texans have been heavily influenced by Bubbling Talkingbirds.
- PROFILES AND PLUMAGE: In flocks, the species tend to stand in a chain of beak to ear to beak, etc. Plumage is variable but is not permitted to cover the ears.
- HABITAT: Found in all offices, but flock particularly at reception desks, bridge tables, bowling alleys, and recreational campgrounds.
- CALL: "Don't quote me, but. . . ."

Bubbling Talkingbirds

Vaga de los Ríos

Vago de los Ríos

👉 Executive Jackasses

- BEHAVIORAL PATTERNS: Like the Laughing Jackass, the Executive Jackass is related to the Giant Kingfisher species. Both males and females fish for reasons to stop whatever is being done or whatever is being planned to be done. The Executive Jackasses fish for flaws no matter how insignificant or irrelevant. Once a flaw is found, the total project will be beaten to death against some minor regulation or a long-forgotten ruling of a long-departed functionary. The species burrows in documents, memoranda, and shredded materials.
- PROFILES AND PLUMAGE: Ready profile; forgotten plumage.
- HABITAT: Though they are found in all bureaucracies, Executive Jackasses are most commonly found in: (1) the higher branches of the U.S. postal tree, (2) in budget offices of all types of bureaucracies, and (3) in program offices of foundations.
- CALL: "Wrong form, wrong format, wrong time, wrong margins. . . ."

Vago de los Rios

👉 Flocking Sportingbirds

- BEHAVIORAL PATTERNS: Flocking Sportingbirds move slowly and randomly in their work, but they fly swiftly and unerringly to the sporting rendezvous. Though some of the species covey, most flock, and the consumers and taxpayers ultimately pay the bill.
- PROFILES AND PLUMAGE: Active.
- HABITAT: Flocking Sportingbirds are on the payrolls of all types of bureaucracies. Corporate bureaucracies, for example, provide haven for Golfbirds (a subspecies) who putter for profit-making projects; academic bureaucracies sustain Golfbirds for Platonic balance; cleribureaucracies provide inspiration for Golfbirds who pursue building-fund contributions on the course; and governmental bureaucracies provide the tax support for golfers who pursue career-rewarding contacts on the course and the 19th holes. Similarly, the species can be found in all other sports and games in all bureaucracies.
- CALL: "Let's goooooooo."

Chapter 17

GENUS
Boxed Pigeons

A genus of bureaucrats
who know what to do,
know how to do it,
want to do it,
but are not given a chance to do it.

🖐 Wilted Ramheads

- BEHAVIORAL PATTERNS: A competent bureaucrat who makes consistent efforts to perform.
- PROFILES AND PLUMAGE: Head in downward position; toes in a grapplistic stance. Wing feathers frayed, tail feathers wilted, and top of head flattened from flying into walls.
- HABITAT: In all bureaucracies.
- CALL: Occasionally issue mournful calls when observing Dodupers or Red Tape Warblers. The sounds are the sounds of a taxpayer: "Ohhhh, no. Ohhh, no."

Concerned Teacherbird

- BEHAVIORAL PATTERNS: A species of academic bureaucrats (acabus) characterized by a usually genuine expression of concern for the educational well-being of little birds that are placed under his or her care in a community nest. Little birds often learn how to play on the concern of Teacherbirds; school administrators usually learn how to extract the last ounce of energy from Teacherbirds for nonteaching assignments; and the communities always learn how to extract total time and energy commitment from teachers with minimal fiscal feeding. Teacherbirds are standard targets of nonteachers who believe they know more about teaching than teachers because they have produced offspring. Some do. Teacherbirds are usually classified as public property.
- PROFILES AND PLUMAGE: Profile, sincere and tired. Plumage, frazzled.
- HABITAT: Academic bureaucracies; all levels.
- CALL: "Please take the PTA notices home to your parents. . . ." Or, "Put your books away, and get out pencil and paper. . . ." Some consistently sing: "Answer questions five, seven, and nine at the end of the chapter."

139

 Shuffling
Timidbirds

- BEHAVIORAL PATTERNS: An adequate performer that lacks confidence both in the home and working environs, the Shuffling Timidbird usually handles a heavy work load but is always fearful of making a mistake. Members of the species insist that superiors approve and clear all work performed even if the superior knows less about the work. When confronted with an uncomfortable situation, the Shuffling Timidbird shuffles paper on top of desks and feet under desks.
- PROFILES AND PLUMAGE: Profile submerged; plumage conservative.
- HABITAT: Found in most offices of bureaucracies where they are the whipping birds of Rulingbirds.
- CALL: "Yes, sir. Thank you, sir."

140

Digitated Nanoseconds

- BEHAVIORAL PATTERNS: Specialists in projecting orbital feedback (at one-billionth of a second) with emphasis on looking to the future by looking back. This species is able to empiricize retrogressive policies by posterioric analysis and computerized indicision. Inconsistencies in flight patterns are common but acceptable since they are developed through computers. In military circles, Digitated Nanoseconds are known as *empirical visionaries.*
- PROFILES AND PLUMAGE: Squattistic profiles; color-coded plumage.
- HABITAT: Most corporate, academic, and governmental offices have Digitated Nanoseconds as pets. Though they are irregularly fed, they are sought after as vital status symbols.
- CALL: "Whrrrrrrrr ummmm sputtttt; whrrrrrrrr ummmm sputtttt."

    (Note: Dr. Sidney Taylor, Research Director of the National Taxpayers Union, has studied the periods of nanosecond thinking that have been given to the doubledippers of Capital Hill. Doubledippers are members of the Congress who receive regular congressional emoluments while also receiving pay as retired military officers.)

Vago de los Ríos

Vago de los Rios

🖘 American Postabirds

- BEHAVIORAL PATTERNS: Employees of the new United States Postal Corporation who, with clipped wings, deliver the mail after it has been automatically processed, mechanically crushed, and orbitally shipped to and from distant sorting centers. Postal patrons who read official press releases rarely recognize the service they read about as being the service they receive.
  (The Canadian relatives of the American Postabirds periodically pause in their postal pursuits to teach their clients how to remember their new postal codes. Based on "Letter-Number-Letter (Space) Number-Letter-Number," Canadians walking down the streets can occasionally be heard singing their postal code jingles. M2S 7C9, for example, may become: "Mix two sugars for a seven club nine," or, "Meet two skiers at seven, car nine."
- PROFILES AND PLUMAGE: Profile, sagging; plumage, beaten.
- HABITAT: Post offices.
- CALL: Postabirds tend to cry with sadness as vast numbers of their colleagues are urged out of the service and as the superstructure grows with geometric plushiness.

142

Chapter 18

GENUS
Frazzletailed Storks

The genus of bureaucrats
who know what to do,
know how to do it,
want to do it,
are given a chance to do it,
and do it.

Vaqo de los Rios

🖐 Harried Storks

- BEHAVIORAL PATTERNS: Harried storks are the only birds who know how to deliver. They are the ultimate action persons in bureaucratic institutions to whom all buck slips and action documents are sent. Very few left; an endangered species.
- PROFILES AND PLUMAGE: Hunched profiles as a result of long hours at small crowded desks. Eyes tired and plumage frazzled. Many scars from being beaten about the head.
- HABITAT: Usually found in small windowless offices that are constantly filled with work orders and other papers. Offices cold in winter, hot in summer. Often provided with a coffee pot in order that no time will be lost in the work that supports the rest of the structure.
- CALL: "I'll take it home tonight. . . ."

144

Chapter 19

Field Note Guidelines for Bureaucrat Watchers

Bureaucrat watching can be an exciting new avocation for bureaucrats and nonbureaucrats around the world. Most bureaucrats have been observers of their colleagues, but few have really seen their colleagues in the full range of behavioral beauty. All that is needed to enable a bureaucratic bureaucrat watcher to see the beauty of a fellow bureaucrat is to recast the personality stimuli into proper interpretative terms.

For example, there is a tendency for most people to think of the trunk of a tree as being brown in color and the leaves as being green. A beginning artist, however, quickly learns that the trunk of a tree is a myriad of hues—a touch of brown, a heavier touch of black and white, a dash of orange, and perhaps a tip of the brush in blue or earth green. The leaves are greens, yellows, white, and other colors. An artist is excited by seeing and responding to the world. It is the interplay of the world's forms, substances, colors, winds, sounds, and smells that can excite an artist. What the world, physical and psychological, says to the artist is what the artist moves to express in art form.

An artist perceives; a psychologist perceives; a

teacher perceives; and, a bureaucrat perceives. For the bureaucrat and the nonbureaucrat, the avocation of bureaucrat watching requires a special opening of the eyes, ears, and mind and heart if the thrill of sighting and insighting is to be experienced. Perception involves more than the mere reception and interpretation of visual stimuli; it involves the full sensing of bureaucrats and their interactions with their environment and other bureaucrats as they play, nest, and occasionally work.

The pleasure derived from bureaucrat-watching will be greatly enhanced by constant observation and by taking copious notes. Would-be ornibureaucratologists should follow the lead of artists and intelligence operatives by always having at hand a pad and pencil with which to make field notes.

New bureaucrat-watchers should organize lunchtime committees that will enable them to share their sightings of passing species. Their observations should be entered immediately in their field notes (often in a little black book). The notes should indicate plumage patterns, head and body profiles, feeding and nesting habits, walking and fluttering profiles, feeding styles, and various mannerisms of the bureaucrats being observed. The *Field Note Guidelines* are one means of helping new bureaucrat-watchers learn how to spot and classify bureaucrats.

If an organized group of bureaucrat-watchers should find itself in controversy about classification of a particular specimen, one of the watchers can be designated *Bureaucrat Verificator (BV)*. The BV can simply approach the specimen under observation, and verify the name of the species and the location of its nesting area. Bureaucrats in some offices, car pools, luncheon groups, and coffee claques elect a Bureaucrat Verificator to serve for a predetermined period of time. Some BVs are elected to be BV-for-a-day.

The position of Bureaucrat Verificator is an honored

146

one, and it is a position that is eagerly sought by both young bushy-headed and old fringe-headed bureaucrats. As a matter of professional courtesy, both male and female bureaucrats under observation quickly and smilingly respond to questions asked by Bureaucrat Verificators. Occasionally, a BV may approach what appears to be a bureaucrat, but instead of the smiling response of a bureaucrat-under-observation may receive the frosty rebuff of pompous phonies who are professional crones or drones.

The Field Note Guidelines can serve as an important educational vehicle, and the field notes can be collected and bound for future memory-browsing. The guidelines should be used with joyous solemnity.

Field Note Guidelines

Behavior Pattern	Feeding Habits	Plumage	Species
When feeding, moves plate to cover dribble spots on table cloth.	Shovelistic	Sparse	
When flocking at conventions, roosts near swimming pool.	Nibblistic	Wind-blown	
Eyes rove about room while talking to other guests at receptions and banquets.	Hoveristic	Sprayed	
Walk with fanniestic movement accompanied by smiles and side glances.	Invitational	Carefully careless	
Constantly at feeding grounds. Incessant bobbing; frames food in protective circle of arms and hands; surveys crowd for possible threatening incursions.	Marathon	Acrylic	
Desk-sleeper. Rare arousals.	Unobservable	Fringeful	

Part III

THE
BOREN QUESTION

Chapter 20

How to Nudge a Bureaucrat

People throughout the world are concerned with the difficulty in wringing a decision or a position out of a bureaucrat. A bad decision or position, once given, is even more difficult to change than to obtain. The problem of the steadfast position has caused consternation to officials of governmental, corporate, religious, and academic bureaucracies as well as to taxpaying citizens. It is an inherent characteristic of bureaucracies.

A family, for example, moves into a new neighborhood, and the husband or wife asks the clerk in the electric power company to establish service to the new house. It is a Thursday and the applicant is told that the power cannot be connected until Monday or Tuesday. Among the household items involved in the move is a freezer with a full load of frozen meat, and the family will lose a substantial investment in food if the electricity is not immediately connected. How can the clerk be motivated to change his mind and get the job done quicker?

Or, a salesperson must make an unexpected business trip. He cannot obtain approval for the trip from his boss, however, because the clearance form for the trip is stuck on the desk of an executive assistant to the boss. A major order may hang in the balance. How can the salesperson make the executive assistant change his stance and place the clearance form before the boss for his approval?

A visitor from another country is assaulted and badly beaten, and an officer in the protocol office of the State Department or Ministry of External Affairs needs to advise the ambassador of the visitor's country of the matter. Because formal notes to foreign ambassadors normally begin with the words, "I have the honor to inform Your Excellency . . . ," the officer wishes to alter the wording. He does not feel comfortable about being pleased to advise an ambassador that one of his nation's citizens has been subjected to a beating.[1] How can the official shake loose an appropriately worded note from the person in charge of notes who insists on the standard note form?

When a bureaucrat has taken a position either on a major issue or a minor ministerial matter, how can he or she be nudged into taking a different position? If the position is to have *no* position, how can a person be twiddled into taking one? How can the seemingly immovable be made to move?

An effective weapon in the battle for decision-making and position adjustment is the *Boren Question*. Designed primarily for bureaucrat-nudging, the Boren Question is: *Will you bet your career on it?* Or, more broadly interpreted: *Are you willing to bet your entire future on the position you are taking?*

It is the Boren view that no more than once in a lifetime will a person bet his or her entire career on any single decision or position. Before bureaucrats will do so, they will adjust their positions or qualify their decisions in such a way as to avoid a final career-betting confrontation. Those who have bet their careers in such

[1]It actually happened . . . in the United States Department of State.

a situation, however, have generally found they no longer had one.

Niccolo Machiavelli, a fifteenth-century bureaucrat who had held numerous posts during a distinguished public service career, bet his career by policy identification with a particular administration. Though recognized by political scientists to be a successful polibu (political bureaucrat), and though remembered for his counsel to Prince Lorenzo, Machiavelli was exiled by the Medici. He bet his career, and lost the test of survival, the ultimate test of bureaucratic success.[2]

Ernest Fitzgerald, an employee of the U.S. Air Force, bet his career when he testified truthfully before a U.S. Senate Committee about the cost overruns on a military project. He bet his career by giving honest answers to committee questions, and his job was abolished by the Air Force. Though a tribunal ultimately ordered his position with the Air Force reinstated, his career in the bureaucracy was not enhanced by his nonteam truthfulness.

When a career wager is made and becomes widely known, the entire bureaucracy quietly bristles with anticipatory excitement. If the career-bettor loses, the loss is usually followed by such administrative actions as job abolition. At this point, the watchdog bureaucrats quickly residuate. Even though the bettor may win the final battle, the other bureaucrats take note of the months and years of painful frustration that are the lot of the bettor, and they tend to quietly resolve to avoid betting their careers with their superiors.

In the quest for promotion and the drive for survival, practitioners of the bureaucratic art avoid career-threatening confrontation. The practitioners are never certain about their ability to gauge the backup or power behind the person who poses the Boren Question. What will he or she do if I call the bet? Is the questioner the

[2]For unrelated reading, see *Andersen's Fairy Tales* (New York: A. L. Burt Company, 1900).

sister or cousin of the organization's big boss? Will the questioner cause a furor in the news media? It is the doubt that blends into fear, plus the love of safety and tranquility, that makes the Boren Question one to be weighed carefully.

For the family seeking to obtain speedy installation of electrical service, the Boren Question can cause the office clerk to make the extra telephone call or take other action that would avoid a career-risking confrontation. By wrapping the Boren Question around the possible loss of a major order, the salesman can move his trip-approval form from the desk of the executive assistant to the desk of the boss. By asking, in essence, the Boren Question, the protocol officer can (and did) alter the wording of the ambassadorial note on the beating of his countryman, from one of a prideful announcement to one of appropriate concern and contrition.

For the bureaucrat, the Boren Question stimulates the reflective pause that usually results in a career-saving change in position. For the taxpayer, the Boren Question brings about the desired change in position that will enable a project to move forward or be halted according to the wishes of the forthright questioner.

The Boren Question, therefore, is the specific articulation of an age-old and usually unspoken test for conformity and confrontation avoidance. While the test is most often used as a means of internal control within a bureaucracy, it can also be a positive means through which action can be stimulated by external forces such as taxpaying citizens. *The avoidance of troubling confrontation is the motivational force behind the Boren Question.*

Chapter 21

When Not to Ask the Boren Question

Imagine that you are driving your car through a heavy rainstorm and, in your hurry to get home, you make an illegal turn. Listening to your favorite music on the radio, you fail to hear the wail of the policeman's siren. It is not until the flashing red lights appear about to crash through your foggy rear window that you are aware that you are being paged. You stop your car, and the towering policeman lumbers through the rain to your window. As you hand him your driver's license, he waves off your first words as you attempt to explain your way out of a ticket. At that moment, you may think of asking the Boren Question: Are you willing to bet your entire police career on giving me this ticket? It is a rather doubtful use of the question. A general rule is: do not ask a policeman the Boren Question, particularly if he is standing in the rain.

Assume that you did not ask the question, were given the ticket, and ordered to appear in court. In the courtroom, you find yourself one of many people who have been waiting and listening for hours to a long series of sad stories being told to the judge. One man becomes belligerent and each retort to the judge results in an increase in his fine. Though the man may finally get the message, he leaves behind a red-faced and angry judge. You are next. This would be another doubtful time to pose the Boren Question.

Similarly, it would not be advisable to pose the question to a nervous robber whose gun hand appears to waver in an uncertain manner. The purpose of the Boren Question is to obtain a change in a decision or position from one that you *do not* want to one that you *do* want. A waving gun in a wavering hand would seem to symbolize sufficient behavioral authority to suggest that the waverer has already made basic career decisions that would not be changed by the Boren Question.

The Boren Question, therefore, should not be employed: (1) when there is little doubt that the bureaucrat to be challenged has a feeling of security and authority, or (2) when the bureaucrat is fully charged with the emotion of anger. The question is most effective when the questioner and the bureaucrat are in an atmosphere that permits the bureaucrat to quietly and tranquilly ponder the full import of the question, and when there is a feeling of bureaucratic insecurity.

If a bureaucrat can shuffle papers or doodle meaningless notes while mentally running an inventory of the cards played and unplayed in the game at hand, he usually decides that the matter under consideration is not of sufficient importance to warrant placing all chips in the middle of the table. On the other hand, if the premeeting state of mind of the preliminary exchanges of the meeting itself have engendered the emotion of anger instead of fear, the typical bureaucratic decision-making processes may be sufficiently clouded to result in steadfast adherence to the original stance. From the taxpayer's standpoint, the bureaucrat may become angry without disastrous effects only if the emotion of fear can be built to a level higher than that of anger.

An angry bureaucrat is a dangerous bureaucrat, because anger may so change the threshold of the bureaucratic cave-in that logic may prevail over psychologic, and reason over mental vacuity. Such a situation so alters the normal bureaucratic pattern that the taxpayer would no longer be able to evaluate properly the ratioistic parameters of the statistical interfacing (sometimes referred to as *odds*) of the new game.

Some taxpaying citizens, through long and often painful experience, become skilled twiddlers of bureaucrats, and can use the Boren Question on career-betting as an effective instrument. If the bureaucrat begins to exhibit anger during the course of a conversation, the taxpayer should retreat to find a new approach that will stimulate the fear receptors.[1] When the probes reveal the fear receptors, the taxpayer should stimulate them firmly but lightly until the time arrives for the asking of the Boren Question.

After the question brings about the action sought by the citizen, he knows from experience that an immediate compliment on the keen insights shown by the bureaucrat temporarily seals the position just gained. To consolidate the favorable action, the citizen subsequently writes carefully constructed letters to the bureaucrat's superiors and to some member of the legislative body to whom the citizen may have made some past political contribution.

Unless the citizen can sense an immediate way to convert bureaucratic anger into bureaucratic insecurity,

[1]Physiologically, the body's neurons have specialized endings, receptors, that are activated by various stimuli. The threshold point is the point at which the stimulus triggers the neuron and causes it to send its impulse to the part of the brain that interprets the particular stimulus. The rods and cones of the eye's retina, for example, are the specialized receptors that are stimulated by light and color. Other specialized receptors are triggered by such stimuli as pressure, heat, sound, and etc. The term "fear receptors" is a borenistic term that uses profound minimalities and scientific puerility to describe the ineffable impingers that activate the nondirective anxiety neurosis.

unless the sense of secure authority can be converted into a fear of losing the authority, and unless the citizen can orchestrate the bureaucratic fear of an either-or type of confrontation, the Boren Question should be reserved for another time.

A chicken never challenges a chef . . . unless the challenge is made while the chicken is roosting over soon-to-be-served bouillabaisse.

Chapter 22

The Boren Question and Committing the Committee

During the earliest stages of the Stone Age, individuals made their decisions in an independent manner. To strike a blow for liberty or for food tended to be a quick decision in response to a simple situation. It was not until the later stages of the Stone Age, that group decision began to appear.

To roam or to remain, to hunt alone or in groups, to build large traps for animals or to merely avoid the animals . . . these were some of the earliest decisions to be made on a group basis. The strong survived, and the strongest became chairman of the committee.

Today, students of bureaucracy watch with hidden glee the worldwide trend to institutionalize all human endeavors. The great surge of bureaucratic growth has ancient and interesting antecedents. The practitioners of the world's oldest profession, for example, were the first to work together in a natural but organized way. They collaborated in matters of location, protection, fees, and marketing, and their marketing coordinators began to develop channels for performance assignments and to establish various liaison relationships. Thus, it was the world's *oldest* profession that gave birth to the world's *second oldest* profession, bureaucracy.

The Magna Carta, forced upon King John in 1215,

159

was the result of the deliberations of a committee of noblemen. The Declaration of Independence of the United States was the result of the committee process, and Bolivar and San Martin moved forward through committee orchestration. Canada, today, is the only nation that officially and effectively meditates, legislates, promulgates, and coordinates in a bilingual manner. Her decisions and reports reflect a new committee culturality.

Committee decision-making procedures have not been altered by the impact of geography or the enrichment of language. The refreshments committee of the Saturday Afternoon Study Club, for example, follows the same basic procedures that were used in the Neanderthalic caves or used by the food preparation committee that served the first Inca, Manco Capac, when he landed on the shore of Lago Titicaca at Puno, Peru. British Parliament, the board of trustees of Peter University, the finance committee of the church, and the burglary ring coordinated out of the White House all have shared common organizational procedures.

Complicated procedures, time for prodigious pondering, loss of records, and diffusion of responsibility have remained as the chief characteristics of the committee process. The usual committee report is what a professional bureaucrat would call "a fuzzification of viable options," or a report that is subject to multiple interpretation.

Once a report has been made and accepted, the recipient of the report must accept full responsibility for whatever action he or she may take. If the action proves to be disastrous, the committee members will quickly rally around one of the interpretations other than the one followed by the recipient of the report. If the action proves to be sound, the committee will take credit for the wisdom of the action.

Committee decisions have been difficult to *defuzzify*,

160

but defuzzification can be accomplished by posing the Boren Question.

Though responsibility may be diffused by the committee process, some effective targeting can be accomplished, because there ultimately must be a person who chaired or cochaired the committee deliberations and who must file the report. Defuzzification can be forced if the recipient of the report handles it in the proper way at the proper time.

When the report is presented by the chairperson, the recipient should clarify his or her understanding of the report in a discussion with the chairperson. On the basis of the clarified position, the chairperson or reporting official should be asked the Boren Question: Are you willing to bet your entire future on the report and our mutual understanding of it? If there is any doubt in the mind of the chairperson, the committee will be called back into session for certain refinement, and the report will be rewritten to conform with what the senior official wants and expects. Thus the committee report is not only defuzzified but also will reflect what the receiver of the report wanted in the first place.

In those rare situations in which the recipient is actually wanting an honest and unbiased report, the Boren Question can help assure that serious study is behind the report. Before a bureaucrat will bet his or her career on a single report, the report must be a serious piece of work. If not, the report will be returned to the committee for "appropriate refinement."

Defuzzification can only be accomplished through the use of the Boren Question. The protective shield of "interpretive adjustivity" can be removed from both the committee and the report recipient who must act upon the committee report, and the Boren Question may have nudged another amorphous mass toward a line of action.

Chapter 23

How History Might Have Been Changed Had the Boren Question Been Asked

The course of history has been influenced by men and women who have made difficult but courageous decisions in times of public turmoil or in moments of quiet inventiveness. For the most part, however, the historical flow[1] has followed the bureaucratic course of least resistance, and has drifted with the consequences of accidental events or casual decisions.

The element of courage makes the Boren Question inoperable, but the element of nonchalant drifting makes the Boren Question a viable mechanism for altering the typical drift of bureaucratic decisions.[2] It is in this sense that posing the Boren Question might have altered the course of history had the question been asked.

Consider the Trojan War, for example. Paris, the

[1] A noted observer of international movements, Brian Beun, made a special study of the historical flow. His report to the Vagolandia Forum of Harpers Ferry in 1971 indicated that the United States policy toward Latin America was "not even in the edge of the historical flow."

[2] Decision-making by drifting can be called *driftative decision-making*. It involves easy drifting with the debris of near-thoughts and almost-logic until the decision is made by the events, whatever they may be, and however they may emerge.

162

son of the king of Troy, had carried off Helen, the wife of Menelaus of Sparta. Some 100,000 troops went to Troy where they laid siege to the city for ten years. They were not able to gain entrance to the city until Greek soldiers were hidden in the interior of a huge wooden horse. Entrance was gained, and Troy was captured, sacked, and burned. If the Boren Question had been asked of the commander who opened the gates to the wooden horse, perhaps the gates would have remained closed, and Troy would not have been captured.

Or recall the decision on the Bay of Pigs invasion. President John F. Kennedy accepted the strong recommendations of Allen Dulles, then director of the Central Intelligence Agency. If President Kennedy had asked Allen Dulles if he, Dulles, were willing to bet his career (and the career of key advisors) on the basic recommendations being made, it is possible that Mr. Dulles might have returned to CIA headquarters to discuss the question again with his advisors. The result could have been a reconsideration of recommendations, and the Bay of Pigs fracasso of April 17, 1961, might have been avoided.

King Ferdinand V of Spain was very cool to the plea for assistance from Columbus, because his kingly efforts were directed at forming a powerful coalition in Europe. Queen Isabella gave her support to Columbus, but what might have happened if King Ferdinand had chauvinistically whirled upon her and said, "Woman, are you willing to bet your entire future on the success of the Columbus scheme?" Is it not possible that Queen Isabella might have chosen a conservative response, thus removing the important support needed for the discovery voyage?

If President Lyndon B. Johnson had asked the Boren Question of his chief military advisor, could the course and extent of United States involvement in Vietnam have been changed?

If the officials of International Telephone and Telegraph had been asked the Boren Question as related to the future of the company, would the intervention in the internal affairs of Chile have taken place?

When decisions were made on alternate courses to sail or alternate directions to take on land, would the more cautious course have been chosen by explorers if the Boren Question had been posed at the moment of decision? Consider how history might have been altered if different decisions had been made by such men as Vasco da Gama, Ferdinand Magellan, John Cabot, Walter Raleigh, Jacques Cartier, Francisco Coronado, or Samuel de Champlain?

If Moses had posed the Boren Question when he was atop Mt. Sinai, is it possible that today we might have eleven commandments or nine commandments instead of ten?

The possible impact of the Boren Question can be pondered as it relates not only to the history of nations but also to the intertwining history of corporations, academic and religious institutions, and the labor movement. If the Justice Department in the United States, for example, had asked the question of corporate officials as they considered certain mergers that had monopolistic colorations, would the giant conglomerates and the international corporations be affecting history as they are today? One has merely to consider the influence of such corporations in the governmental affairs of Latin American nations and the oil-rich nations of the Middle East to sense the possible impact the Boren Question might have had if it had been posed at the appropriate time by a forceful Justice Department. Today, however, the corporate structures have grown so strong that corporate courage has entered the picture, and the impact of the Boren Question tends to bring forth amused smiles instead of a change in stance.

Perhaps, of course, there may come a time when

key decision-makers for nations may relate the question to one of national direction. "Do we, as a nation, want to bet all the heritage of the past, all the human and material wealth of our nation at present, and all the human aspirations of this generation and the freedom of future generations on the course we are now pursuing? Are we, as a nation, willing to bet the lives of our people on a national policy of *driftative decision-making*, the decision-making by drift? Are we, as a nation, willing to settle into a Neanderthalic nest and wrap ourselves in the red tape that binds us together as an immovable force for the steadfast status quo?"

Oh, 'tis consummation devoutly to be pondered. After all, what is history but a collection of little stories? Or, what is history but the forward look of contemporary bureaucrats?

Part IV

WORDS FROM THE BOREN BIRDCAGE

Chapter 24

Marginal Ponderings

Recognition of one's own ignorance immediately disqualifies one from becoming a congressman, a college dean, or a bureaucrat.

If you want to find out what's on a bureaucrat's mind, don't ask him. It could embarrass him.

A geometrical bureaucrat is one who is always figuring the angles.

Bureaucrats do not oppose innovation, as long as it is innovation within established guidelines.

Business bureaucracy is becoming a conglomerated mess.

Grumbling is for amateurs; analyzing is for professionals.

Bureaucrats know that there is no place for littleness as they serve as stewards of the taxpayers' dollars. That is why they round off figures to the nearest billion.

The fee paid for the services of a bull is not based on how long the bull works but on the quality of the work performed. A bureaucrat, on the other hand, is paid not for the quality of work but the time that it takes to do whatever it is that a bureaucrat is assigned to do—if anyone can remember whatever it was that the bureaucrat was originally assigned to do.

Bureaucrats know that new ideas are uncomfortable, but old ideas, like old shoes, comfort both body and spirit.

A study of the minutes of the executive committees of major corporations suggests that the practice of conceptual celibacy is well-established in the higher echelons of the corporate world. An extended period of celebated leadership is rarely joyously celebrated by stockholders.

Proficient practitioners of moderated honesty and adjustive integrity are rarely proficient survivors.

A bureaucrat giving birth to a new idea is like a mule giving birth to a horse.

Bureaucrats always keep a fearful eye on the people, because some day the people might decide to take over the government.

Academic bureaucrats have demonstrated that a person need not be pompous to be a bureaucrat, but it helps.

A stockholder knows less about corporate operations than a taxpayer knows about government. Corporation executives believe that taxpayers should run the government, but that stockholders should leave corporate affairs to management.

Mumbling the formula of rigid procedures and chanting the prohibitions of restrictive regulations comprise the principal incantations of all professional bureaucrats.

Bureaucratic lead time is not measured in days, weeks, or months, but in fiscal years.

The legal officers of organizations are usually very literate people. Quoting from their books, they can litter the path of problem-solving proposals with enough preventive citations to keep things from happening until the problem goes away or submerges the organization. If the organization is submerged, the legal officers can cite their way through bankruptcies, phase-outs, reorganizations, or acquisitions.

When the three-dollar bill is established, the politician will design it, the bureaucrat will spend it, and the taxpayer will foot the bill.

Politicians compromise; bureaucrats fold.

Some bureaucrats get ahead by plodding, others by plotting. The plod-plot axis is sometimes tilted by too much plotting, and the plodders get the short end of the stick. This is known as the *bureaucratic shaft*.

The rule for becoming a successful phoney is a simple one: If you are going to be a phoney, be sincere.

There are many genuine phonies in large organizations, but there are few who are sincere about their phoniness. The difference between genuine phonies and sincere phonies is that the genuine phonies may never recognize their phoniness, but the sincere phonies are aware of being phonies—and adopt phoniness as a way of life.

Bureaucrats are the ones who keep the wheels of government humming. It's the process of orbital humbuggery.

A mumble and a smile can never be quoted.

Seasoned managers know that milestones can become millstones.

Washington is the flophouse of bureaucracy.

The greatest threats to bureaucracy are those that develop when people get the idea that they should have a voice in the peoples' business. The threats rarely develop, however, because people tend to leave the peoples' business to the bureaucrats who are convinced that they know what is best for the people anyway.

Bungling politicians often become mumbling bureaucrats. The process is called defeat and appointment.

When bureaucrats or politicians are confronted with something they don't understand, they rise above it with mumblistic disdain. Ignorance is successfully conferred by the haughty imperiousness of politicians and the pompous imperviousness of bureaucrats.

A bureaucracy may complete a few projects but it never completes its work.

Great talents are preserved in bureaucracies: wrapped in red tape and submerged in procedural formaldehyde.

History is the forward look of contemporary bureaucrats.

Diplomacy is the highest form of bureaucracy. Its practitioners, the diplomats, are eloquent articulators of marginal thoughts, masterful artisans in issue avoidance, and graceful dancers of the coctailian ballet.

The power of a bureaucrat lies in the strength of his infallible inaction.

A dynamic bureaucrat is one who gestures vigorously while saying nothing.

Bureaucrats should learn to control their anger. If they don't, they could forget to mumble, and they might say something that makes sense.

The simple pleasures of bureaucracy are found in intricate patterns of dysfunctional complexity.

172

Dictionaries and bureaucrats are full of words, and both are developed to be used by others.

One of the biggest dangers that confronts a bureaucrat is the danger of a faltering outlook on life. From time to time a bureaucrat can be caught up in the conversational enthusiasm of accomplishing some task and, if not careful, actually may take some action. Only steadfast adherence to the principles of dynamic inaction and unfaltering devotion to yesbuttisms can save the bureaucrat from the danger of doing something.

The ego of a political bureaucrat is like the product of bubblegum art. It grows larger and thinner until it finally pops, and it leaves a sticky mess.

Upon receiving the Ph.D. degree, many academic bureaucrats wrap their brains in cobwebs and settle down to mental retirement. Some become administrators.

There are more phonies in capital cities than in any other cities of the world. They are not the bureaucrats but those who seek governmental favors.

The furrowed brow of a bureaucrat usually does not mean that there is concern about some problem. The furrowed brow is a well-known bureaucratic mask that can gain temporary protection from someone who may wish to make a thoughtful incursion into the bureaucrat's state of nonthinking serenity and free-floating tranquility.

If it's worth saying, it's worth mumbling.

Politicians are bureaucrats at heart. They don't deal in forms, but they deal in thousands of nonquestion questionnaires with which they update their mailing lists. They lovingly shuffle their index cards listing supporters, and buck constituent mail to agency bureaucrats for noncommittal answers that will be transmitted with a noncommittal letter to the constituent in the hope of obtaining a commitment for political support.

The pattern of bureaucracy is determined by the putter of bureaucrats.

Bureaucrats can accept the management-by-objective concept as long as they remember that the objectives should be fuzzified. Fuzzification of objectives speed their adoption, because everyone can interpret them to mean what they want them to mean.

A leader in a bureaucracy is the person who can convince others that: (1) there's no place worth going, and (2) they should drag up a chair and join the others who aren't going.

A creative bureaucrat is one who can find new ways of saying no.

Why do honest bureaucrats tend to be afraid of dishonest politicians?

Professional bureaucrats do not oppose cutting red tape . . . as long as it is cut lengthwise.

An honest thought is the most highly classified thing in any bureaucracy.

Bureaucracy is as immortal as time itself.

The only time bureaucrats use short sentences and simple words is when they are devitalizing another bureaucrat's work.

The general was a great bureaucrat! I once saw him when he discovered a simple project. He pounced on it like a cat and immediately profundicated it.

At one time, bureaucrats closely studied politicians. They marveled at the interplay of ideas and the flourishes with which they were presented. Today, the ideas have been lost, but bureaucracy has adopted the flourishes.

The perfect memo has never been written. It is always possible to add complexity and marginal thoughts to any message.

Politicians with weak arguments win by vocal intimidation, and bureaucrats win by policy homogenization.

Many politicians make their decisions on public issues by the weight of their mail in pounds rather than the weight of the mail in logic. Most bureaucrats, when forced to make decisions, make them on the basis of diffused responsibility rather than on the basis of correctness.

GLOSSARY

Acabu (ackaboo) An academic bureaucrat. A specialized class of professional bureaucrat (probu) that can be found nesting in institutions of elementary, secondary, and higher education. Most acabus tend to flock together after employment hours and combine flocking and clucking activities. Acabus are among the world's greatest cluckers and regardless of the stated reason for flocking together, they always end up clucking about school policies on grading, teacher's salaries, and innovative methods of appearing to be doing the same old thing in new ways. In most institutional nesting areas, acabus are divided into administration-supporters and administration-nonsupporters. The division is reflected in the patterns of flocking in cafeterias, faculty meetings, and bridge circles.

Bureaucrat Originally a term used to refer to an employee of a government bureau. Today, the term is used to refer to any person who loves red tape, postpones decisions, shuffles paper, and can find many reasons for not doing anything. In professional terms, the bureaucrat seeks to optimize the creative status quo by applying the principles of dynamic inaction, by orbitally dialoguing, by orchestrating patterns of decision postponement, and by mumbling with professional eloquence. Bureaucrats are found in governmental, corporate, academic, religious, and other institutionalized forms of human endeavor.

179

Bureaucratic Movement, The The flow of bureaucracy from capital cities to other parts of the respective nations. Known in the capital cities as *The Movement;* known in other parts of the nation as The BM of (the capital city). Thus, The BM of Washington; The BM of Ottawa, and etc. . . .

Clergicats A professional or in-house term for very liberal cleribureaucrats.

Cleribureaucrats Bureaucrats of institutional religions and religious institutions.

Echosultant A specialized consultant who tells the client what the client wishes to hear. Based on the cautious use of ditto-analysis, echosulting is used extensively by senior officials in all bureaucracies to gain support for weak positions. Echosultants are skilled listeners, keen observers, and profundicating rewriters.

Ego-halo The halo worn and seen by professional bureaucrats who possess maximized egos. Taxpayers and amateur bureaucrats cannot see the ego-halos, but they can sense their existence. Professional bureaucrats (probus) with ego-halos can see those of other probus, and they often become engaged in polite jockeying to casually but deliberately place their ego-halos above all others. Possessors of ego-halos are particularly susceptible to drowning, because many of them believe that they can walk on the sea of bureaucratic molasses.

Haque A bureaucratic noun that is related to the term *hack* (as in political hack), but is distinguished from hack by the professional level of its articulation. Amateurs can become hacks but only a sophisticated professional can become a haque. See *Haque, to.*

Haque, to A bureaucratic verb form to denote the activities of a practicing haque. To haque, therefore, is to perform the function of a haque. See *Haque.*

Haughticality The level of maximized haughtiness. Haughticality relates to the state of haughtiness that has more class than simple or boorish haughtiness. Similarly, to be haughtical is to be haughty with class and style.

-istic A bureaucrats' suffix to indicate planned or purposeful characteristics. Thus, *mumblistic* indicates planned mumbling, rather than accidental or random mumbling; *thrummistic* indicates purposeful thrumming; and, *fuzzistic* indicates planned fuzziness.

Linear mumbling The translocation of multiple tonal patterns that reflect the bold irresolution of a speaker. Prevailing intonations are not distinguishable in word form but extended linear mumbling is usually enhanced by linking tonal patterns with an occasional word or phrase. To the casual listener, linear mumbling may sound like muttering but there is a significant distinction between the two. Muttering is characterized by anger, mumbling by joy.

Mumblesce (mumble-ess) Effervescent and bubblistic elevation of mumbling with positive-poetic overtones. When a bureaucrat mumblesces, the listeners are thrilled by the nonmessage linkage of words of beauty. A nonmumblescer, for example, might greet a dinner partner with, "It's great to be with you." A mumblescer would say, "To be in your presence is to be lifted to supernal heights of joy and inspiration—inspiration that rises from the depths of one's heart to the ultimate level of communicative ineffability." Religious bureaucrats, prospecting male chauvinists, and writers of grant proposals are noted mumblescers; journalists are notoriously poor mumblescers.

Nosistic (nose-istic) Purposeful nose directiveness. Many probus sight down their noses when clucking a message to bureaucrats they believe to be uncouth or inferior in some manner. Purposeful nose-aiming is also practiced in silence. Nosistic gazing can be regularly observed being practiced by officials of the U.S. Department of Housing and Urban Development, by inspectors in municipal licensing offices, and by waiters in French restaurants.

Ornibureaucratology The study of bureaucrats, both amateur and professional bureaucrats who are practitioners of the art in all types of bureaucracies. Ornibureaucratologists study the work, play, feeding, and nesting patterns of bureaucrats, while bureaucratologists also include the study of institutional interfaces and the broader implications of policies and philosophies as they relate to the bureaucratic movement. Ornibureaucratology is to bureaucratology as ornithology is to zoology.

Pastify Bureaucratic verb form. The process of aging something through adjustive interpretation. Viz., instantly antiquing a concept.

Polibu (poly-boo) Political bureaucrat which tends to wrap its body in flaggistic materials and use other accoutrements of the national spirit. Polibus are a specialized type of probu whose species roost primarily in capitols and city halls. Dialogues are intonations of compromise and accommodation. Public pronouncements are directed down the beak to constituents and are characterized by loud and nonmessage bugling. Beginning polibus tend to move forcefully and decisively but experiential maturity converts such action into straddlistic accommodation. Polibus are outstanding profundicators and orbital dialoguers.

Posicator A person who is a professional poser of questions. Most posicators are marathon mumblers and orbital dialoguers who can link dependent clauses for effective prolongation of questions. Posicators pose questions and never answers . . . unless, of course, the answer is in the form of another question.

Probu (pro-boo) A professional bureaucrat; a bureaucrat who has mastered the skills of orbital dialoguing, decision postponement, and articulate mumbling. All probus are dedicated to the principles of dynamic inaction and creative nonresponsiveness.

Probuistic A purposeful or programmed plan or activity that is coordinated by a professional bureaucrat. All bureaucratic processes tend to be beautiful, but some of them may evolve from random activity of nonbureaucrats or haphazard planning by an amateur bureaucrat. All things probuistic must be the product of a professional bureaucrat.

Profundicator A person who can translate simple ideas and concepts into semantical echo patterns that enrich the tonal qualities of idea articulation while optimizing the ineffability of minimal and marginal thought processes. Mere laymen tend to equate profundication with obfuscation, but professional bureaucrats and bureaucrat watchers view obfuscation as an unprofessional term that does not reflect the philosophical depth of profundication.

The terms *profundicator* and *profundifier* mean the same thing, as is the case of *profundication* and *profundification*. The difference lies in the acculturated origin of the user. Graduates of state universities and agricultural colleges tend to use the bureaucratic verb *profundicate* while graduates of Ivy League institutions tend to use the bureaucratic verb *profundify*.

Putteristic Planned or programmed puttering as distinguished from unplanned or random puttering (see-*istic*).

Residuate A bureaucratic verb form that refers: (1) to maintaining a low profile; and (2) to sit, rest, or squatulate while maintaining a low profile. A residual profile is the

182

lowest of low profiles and is widely used by employees in all bureaucracies during time of stress or turmoil. Residuum-related, the term is used almost exclusively in bureaucratic circles.

Rumperatory Relating to lagging portions of anatomical, semantical, or organizational entities. A rumperatory pat, for example, usually refers to a light slap on the lagging part of the anatomy. A rumperatory comment is an expression of an afterthought. Old-time bureaucrats often refer to rumperatory comments as the rumbleseat of thought. Applied to organizational matters, the term is used in reference to last-minute and crisis-oriented establishment of new committees, blue ribbon commissions, and coordinating offices. Rumperatory offices often appear on the fringes of organizational charts; they are placed there because no other place exists for them. Rumperatory offices tend to evolve into permanent governmental agencies, new corporate staff divisions, or schools of academic studies.

Vertical mumbling The highest form of the mumbling art. Vertical mumblers are outstanding masters of maximizing word strings that reflect both conceptual celibacy and multisyllabitic intonations. Bureaucrats who can mumble with verticality usually receive promotions, elevated titles, and professional respect from their colleagues, because no one can understand with certainty what they are saying. Vertical mumblers who can use long word strings, and who can project the feeling of sincerity, eventually bubble to the top of the various bureaucracies in which they may be found. The State Department and the Pentagon serve as the graduate schools of the mumbling art.